# THE DUCK
# A DIRTY LA

# The Duck with a Dirty Laugh

More family adventures in rural France

by Anne Loader

Illustrated by Patricia Kelsall

An imprint of
ANNE LOADER
PUBLICATIONS

Dedicated with love to
**Jules and Berthe**
**Marcel and Jacqueline Simon**
**Roger and Eileen Williamson**

ISBN 1 901253 35 X
Published with full colour cover
and minor updating in July 2003

First published December 1999
(Original ISBN 1 901253 09 0)

Published by:
Léonie Press
an imprint of
Anne Loader Publications
13 Vale Road, Hartford,
Northwich, Cheshire CW8 1PL
Gt Britain
Tel: 01606 75660   Fax: 01606 77609
e-mail: anne@aloaderpubs.u-net.com
Website: http://www.aloaderpubs.u-net.com

Printed by:
Anne Loader Publications
Collating and binding by: B & S Swindells Ltd., Knutsford
Cover lamination by: The Finishing Touch, St Helens

# About the author and illustrator

**Anne Loader** is a writer and publisher. She was born in Lincolnshire in 1948 and trained as a journalist with East Midland Allied Press. In 1969 she married Jack Loader who was doing a PhD at Southampton University. She worked at the *Southern Evening Echo* until the couple moved to Cheshire in 1970 when Jack started work as a research scientist in the chemical industry. They had two sons and for the next ten years Anne worked from home as a writer and printer. She edited and contributed to *Pregnancy and Parenthood* on behalf of The National Childbirth Trust, which was published by OUP in 1980. The same year she returned to journalism as a feature writer on *Northwich World* and in 1984 she helped to start the *Crewe and Nantwich Guardian,* becoming editor in 1985. She was made redundant as editor in 1995 and in 1996 she set up as a freelance writer and page designer. Shortly afterwards, she started the Léonie Press as an imprint of Anne Loader Publications, specialising in producing books on local history and autobiography. Her first book about France, *A Bull by the Back Door,* published in October 1997, was widely acclaimed. Extracts were serialised in *Living France* magazine. Following the success of *The Duck with a Dirty Laugh* in 1999 she wrote the third instalment, *The Bells of St Paradis* in 2001.

**Patricia Kelsall** is a part-time lecturer in Art & Design at Mid-Cheshire College teaching drawing and painting to full-time and part-time students. She has exhibited her work mainly in the North East of England and in Cheshire as well as the Royal Academy in London, the Manchester Academy of Fine Art and at the Annual Salon in Mornant, France. Patricia's illustrations and paintings have appeared in numerous publications including Newcastle 900 by Frank Graham, greetings card designs for Bucentaur Gallery and many limited edition publications including publicity brochures, letterheads, menus and local authority town trail leaflets. Her paintings have been reviewed in *The Observer Magazine* and *The Guardian* newspaper. She has done many of the illustrations for books published by Anne Loader, including *A Bull by the Back Door* and *The Bells of St Paradis,* and undertakes many private commissions. Patricia loves visiting France and she and her artist husband Richard have spent many Summer holidays in France where they enjoy walking combined with outdoor sketching and painting.

# The Duck with a Dirty Laugh

Everything described in this book is true, to the best of my knowledge, and based on our diaries. However to protect the privacy of our friends in France I have changed their names and the names of the villages mentioned (except for Mornant). They were kind to us because they are marvellous people — not because they thought they would be the subjects of a book. We thank them from the bottom of our hearts.

I have mentioned my beloved mother's sad affliction with Alzheimer's Disease because this book is about real life. What was happening to her dominated almost every waking moment for us during the timespan described. We knew nothing about the condition when we first had to cope with it and felt extremely vulnerable. Perhaps what I have written may help others in the same situation to know that they are not alone in their pain.

Anne Loader

# List of illustrations

i

# Contents

*Our visitors were like members of the family*

# Introduction

**M**ilord stood on the doormat and pushed at the heavily carved front door until it opened. Then he trotted into the kitchen, cocked his leg against the buckets stacked under the porcelain sink and investigated the waste-bin.

His brother Max followed, too shy to make his mark so blatantly on someone else's territory. His target was usually one of the hubcaps of our Peugeot estate outside.

Last of all was Gitane, squirming with anticipated pleasure from the tip of her brown nose to the end of her feathered tail: a shining example of canine cupboard love in its most endearing and shameless form.

They had gathered as always on the concrete path bordering the main front entrance to our Limousin farmhouse. It was time for doggy elevenses.

Sometimes we answered their daily scratches on the door by putting out bowls of leftovers from our meals. At other times they were lucky. The catch on the 200-year-old oak door was dodgy. It was liable to succumb to paw pressure. If we weren't in the big beamed kitchen they had the run of the place to themselves — until we heard the patter of feet on the tiles.

The puddles of piddle annoyed us but mostly we were pleased to see our visitors. They were like members of the family. We had left our own much-loved dogs at home in Cheshire and we missed them terribly. We couldn't wait until the quarantine laws were changed so that they could come to France too.

While St Paradis was a heaven on earth for us, we knew it was also a dog's nirvana. In other places we'd seen many French dogs chained up, cowed and bored witless. St Paradis was so far off the beaten track that its dog population outnumbered the daily car census. We simply didn't get passing motorists — unless they were hopelessly lost. All the local people knew about Milord, Max, Gitane and her daughter Soupette. They'd known and loved Betty too, who, before her premature death from an infection had spent most of her life lying quite safe in the centre of the road outside her house. And there had been the sheepdog Lassie, whose loss as a longtime companion still troubled our old friend Michel.

Round the corner was the senile black farm dog, whose mangy hair had almost dropped out, and his younger and more aggressive companion who chased any car impertinent enough to venture past his barn.

Caesar, the impeccably-behaved Alsatian, was a frequent visitor, sometimes accompanied by a perky little friend called Daisy who'd survived an appalling farm accident and now trotted round on her three remaining legs.

Then there were the villagers' hunting dogs — at least a dozen — whose baying and excited barks were an integral part of the backdrop of sounds in St Paradis, especially at mealtimes or when they were raring to go out with the *chasseurs*.

Lastly were the occasional marauders, outsiders who had not been trained from birth to leave the livestock and poultry alone, like the one who killed The Duck with a Dirty Laugh as he told rude jokes to his friends on the pond.

Few of St Paradis' dogs led pampered lives. They ate kitchen scraps and when their owners or human acquaintances laid down the law they obeyed, usually without question. Milord and Max knew all about their mistress's sharp tongue and the switch she wielded when they were naughty.

But they had the run of the roads and the fields. The village was theirs to wander and possess. There were rats to chase and cats to intimidate. They had wonderful scents to sniff and foul substances to roll in. Most dogs in the world would have swapped roles with them without a second thought.

And our three visitors knew that the easy-touch English couple kept a box of dog biscuits, just for them, in the back kitchen. All they had to do was ask nicely.

A St Paradis without dogs was unimaginable. As unimaginable as a St Paradis without its families of bulls with their cows and calves — or the music of birdsong and farm machinery from dawn till dusk.

**St Paradis**
**May 1998**

2

# Chapter One – May 1996

John Steinbeck once wrote that you couldn't mend a car without cutting yourself and making a libation of blood to the gods. It seemed to be the same with St Paradis and me.

I'd had a sprained wrist, mastitis, an infected insect bite and various other ailments and injuries, either in our French haven or just before going. It was uncanny. Normally I was boringly healthy. Any problems seemed to be confined to high blood pressure which was kept comfortably at bay with daily tablets, and an annual cold.

I'd also been made redundant within a day or two of returning home from a particularly idyllic St Paradis holiday. It seemed that Fate made us pay for the exquisite privilege of having our lives enhanced by the place.

A couple of weeks before we set out for the Limousin in early May 1996 we took our five dogs for their usual walk round a reclaimed waste tip in Northwich which had been transformed into woodland and open fields. Packed into the back of the Peugeot were Sally, fat as a black barrel, part sheepdog and part Labrador; Jazz, thin as a red rake, our young Irish Setter; and the stately deaf Lady, our 15-year-old Setter. We'd rescued them all at different times from different fates. Darting between them and fizzing with energy were Sally's accidental offspring, golden Goldie and black-and-white Ziggy, who were more than two years old but were still referred to universally as "the pups". Ziggy's main pleasure in life was tormenting her brother and dragging him round with her teeth embedded in his collar.

The five jumped out of the boot and spread out. As I turned away after shutting the tailgate, Ziggy made a dive for Goldie's throat. She shot behind my legs, collapsing the knee joints like a closing hinge and throwing me heavily to the ground. I caught the projecting bumper all the way down.

Lying on the dusty car park, winded, I was conscious of a lot of pain in my side and back. It hurt to breathe.

"Are you all right?" asked my husband Jack.

"I think I've broken my ribs," I replied. Then I cried.

*All the poultry traders were clustered round the steps of the church*

Next day I consulted the doctor. He said I hadn't fractured anything but was badly bruised. He added that even if I'd cracked my ribs there wasn't much I could do about it except swallow painkillers and let nature take its course. It would be OK after a month to six weeks.

"Marvellous!" I thought.

I couldn't laugh because it hurt too much. I could only just breathe and coughing or sneezing were a horrible prospect. Speech wasn't much fun either. So I smiled at him — ironically.

"Typical!" I whispered to Jack that night. "Wouldn't you just *know* that we were going to St Paradis?"

We have always been incredibly lucky. Many of our friends and relatives regard us as a "good home" for items of furniture or domestic equipment that they want to get rid of but for sentimental reasons can't bring themselves to take to the tip. The house in France is almost entirely furnished this way, with a few second-hand or sale bargains of our own thrown in.

The throwing-in is the problem.

Getting all our treasured junk to St Paradis is a perennial nightmare whenever we need to pack the trailer. We have far more stuff than we can transport.

Jack and I have different ideas about the capacity of the 6ft x 4ft trailer. I work on the female principle that if I want things to go to France badly enough — like a three-seater settee, a dismantled fitted kitchen, two sinks, two bicycles and a Victorian writing desk — they can surely be "fitted in somewhere". Jack envisages the trailer filled with all the tools and woodworking equipment which he considers essential and any empty corners stuffed with practical things like bags of compost or rolls of fibreglass insulation.

Like good caravanners we weigh the trailer towbar on our bathroom scales and adjust the weight accordingly.

We always reach a compromise.

We invariably squeeze in more than he imagined and less than I imagined.

And half-way to Portsmouth we remember what we have forgotten.

We usually did the packing the night before we left and had learned from experience that this was not good for the temper. On this occasion we decided to load the trailer several days in advance — especially as I was completely useless as a native porter.

A friend of Jack's had kindly given us a complete fitted kitchen with beige effect doors and dark oak details. We had worked out that with a bit of modification it would go perfectly into the back kitchen at St Paradis. We had collected it, dismantled, from their home and written in pencil on each component piece, describing more or less what it was. There was a larder unit, three top cupboards, two base units and a stainless steel sink — but no working surfaces. We had looked at working surfaces in the local DIY stores but they were too heavy to carry on the roof-rack and we decided to buy one in France. Sadly, we thought there was no room for the base unit and sink in the trailer and left them behind.

We'd also been given a very large and attractive IKEA sofa by some other friends but it would have completely dominated the trailer on its own. It was destined for the upstairs study at St Paradis — which was to be my decorating project during this stay — but I knew I couldn't help Jack carry it up the stairs with my ribs in their present condition.

We set off on May 9 at 4pm and arrived at the port at 8.35pm, an hour early. This was a record. When we joined the M6 at Holmes Chapel we found the traffic going in three parallel lanes at 60mph, with none of the stop/start bunching which usually made the journey so unbearable.

Around Oxford we remembered that we had forgotten the oak trees.

Knowing that you are not supposed to introduce foreign species of plants to France, we bring back acorns from St Paradis, nurture them in plant pots at home and then take them back for replanting round the edges of the field when they are sufficiently sturdy.

The current batch was still resplendent on the staging in our Hartford garden.

We disembarked from the ferry at Le Havre at 7.15am the next morning having had to wait for the crew to find the owners of an unoccupied car which had blocked in scores of passengers. We had an uneventful journey but noted that all the toll prices had increased since our last visit in January.

When we arrived at St Paradis the first thing we noticed was that our dear old friend Paul, who lives opposite and cares for the house as a labour of love, had made a rockery for us at the front with heavy blocks of granite all precisely lined up against a piece of string. The back garden, which fills with rampant nettles, brambles and weeds as soon as we turn our backs, had been cleared completely and was now just neatly raked soil. We were delighted but concerned that a man now well into his eighties should have done so much hard physical work on our behalf.

When we examined the mail which Paul had left on the kitchen table we knew we had really been accepted by our adopted country: we discovered a very special prize offer, exclusively for us, M et Mme Loader, from the *Reader's Digest*!

We went over to greet Paul and his Dutch partner Elisabeth and to announce our arrival. Michel, a retired farmer from down the road and a great friend of Paul's, was there too. Panic had gripped England and France in the wake of Mad Cow Disease and it was an obvious topic of conversation here in the middle of cattle farming country. French housewives were turning away from beef in general and the Limousin was beginning to suffer.

Michel was suffering personally too. His sheepdog, Lassie had very recently died from breast cancer and he was bereft. He said he was too old to have a new dog but losing Lassie was like losing a member of the family. She'd dogged his heels wherever he walked and sat companionably with him in tractor or trailer. Unlike some other farm dogs we knew, she had always been welcomed by his wife in their spacious kitchen and had spent many hours dozing on the mat near the woodburning cooker. There would be a conspicuous gap there now.

Paul told us that the skylight in our attic had been damaged in a storm and that he had asked his daughter-in-law's builder boyfriend, Martin, to mend it for us. We were very grateful. Even when it had lain empty for years, the house had remained weatherproof.

He also said that during his clearing work on the back garden, he had pulled the creeper off the side of the henhouse and discovered a door hidden behind it. He'd managed to get it open and found a perfectly good, hand-made wheelbarrow, which he was sure would come in handy, inside a previously unknown part of the building.

We gave Paul and Elisabeth some little thank-you presents for looking after the house. We knew that Paul went in every day to open the shutters and air the rooms as well as doing all sorts of jobs outside. One present was a rechargeable torch — common at home but rare and expensive in France at the time. We had four — two in England and two which we'd brought to St Paradis. Like everyone in the hamlet the couple got through many torch batteries each winter as the street lighting was unreliable and the nights were pitch black — an astronomer's delight but not so delightful if you wanted to walk anywhere under the bright stars.

Back at the house we popped a pizza in the oven, put an ergonomic knobbly foam mattress on our rather uncomfortable double bed, had a quick supper and collapsed onto the comforting knobbles, shattered.

We slept fitfully. The granite walls still retained the cold which had been stored there since the winter. We had a digital maximum-minimum thermometer in the kitchen which recorded the temperatures inside and out, and we knew from experience that when it was inhabited the house warmed up at about a degree Centigrade a day. Just now it was decidedly chilly.

However, it was so beautifully built and designed that it wasn't damp. The 18th and 19th century masons of the Limousin were deservedly famous throughout France for the quality of their workmanship and our house was a shining example of their craft. Its perfect humidity had preserved letters, books and documents for 100 years without a speck of mould or distortion of the paper. It naturally possessed the qualities which modern museums strive for.

We had been thrilled to find relics of former occupiers which brought the whole history of the house to life. The only problem was that it was designed by masons who wore a lot more clothes than we did. They would have greeted Thermolactyl underwear as a major life-enhancing breakthrough.

Next morning we saw Martin's lorry outside Paul and Elisabeth's house and went over to see him. We paid him for his work — he said he'd mended the skylight and replaced some of the metal flashing on the ridge of the house roof. Jack showed him another repair which needed to be done on the barn roof — far too high for our ladder to reach and beyond the height that he felt safe anyway. Martin said it would be easy and he would do it when he had the time.

We drove into the nearest town to do some essential shopping. The local grocers cum not-very-super market had been acquired by a national franchise and was completely transformed. Previously you'd endured grumpy service, high prices, poor quality goods and very little choice but now the premises were modern, the staff welcoming, the stock interesting and the prices more competitive.

We knew that the new local mayor had campaigned on the issue of providing a supermarket and a petrol station for the town and wondered if he was partly responsible.

In the streets the traders were getting ready for one of the major local events — the massive horse fair to be held the following day. It was almost a national event and we were looking forward to going for the first time.

Back home we started work on the kitchen units. We assembled the larder unit, put a chipboard back on it to keep out the mice and painted white primer on the backing. Then we did the same with the high cupboards.

A fireguard Jack had made to fit in front of the steel pipe dog-grate in the enormous Limousin *cantou* fireplace slotted in exactly. We wanted to protect the nearby furniture and floor-covering from flying sparks and burning bits of wood that might roll off the grate. We had lit the fire because it looked warm and welcoming but most of the heat went up the vast chimney and we were still so cold that we wore our body-warmers indoors — in May…

While I made a Balti supper in the wok, Jack sprayed weed-killer on the parts of the garden Paul had not tackled and strimmed the grass round the front of the house and barn. While he was doing this, Paul brought his Dutch brother-in-law over to see what we were doing. He was a very interesting man of our own age who had been a power engineer on oil rigs all over the world. A year before we'd spent a very pleasant evening with him and his wife and we were embarrassed that we couldn't pronounce his name. We hadn't seen it written down and to the uninitiated it sounded like a clearing of the throat. Paul couldn't say it either and had long ago re-christened him "Hugo". Rather ashamed, for it didn't seem right not to make the linguistic effort, we adopted the same pseudonym.

After our Balti we went to bed early; exhausted.

Next morning we had breakfast and tried to listen to Radio Four but were driven mad by the rhythmical interference from an electric fence which was keeping a group of white cows enclosed in a field close by. We tidied up and set off for the horse fair. The skies were grey and we were glad of our anoraks when a persistent misty drizzle started.

Not knowing what to expect, we were surprised to find the roads lined with parked cars quite a distance from the town centre and a long way from the arena where the horses would be sold. We parked near the football pitch and joined the throng of people walking down the middle of the street. We were used to seeing only local number-plates but soon spotted that the parked vehicles came from all over the country.

At the top of the hill we came to one of the main crossroads and found that the festivities began there. We had expected only horses to be for sale but it was obvious that the event was an excuse for a massive jamboree of selling — the market to end all markets.

To our left we could see colourful stalls on both sides of the street which led to the usual market square and to our right, towards the medieval heart of the town, we could hear a cacophony of clucks, quacks, cheeps and chirps. We decided to investigate these first.

We found a row of traders with big wire cages full of live birds and a few rabbits which they had brought to the market in lorries.

Yellow plastic crates for transporting this livestock were stacked everywhere.

There were hundreds of baby birds — geese, chickens, ducks and turkeys — and young adults of the same species. As far as we could tell, they weren't being bought immediately for the pot but to replenish stocks. Even if they no longer farmed for a living, most country people in the area had enough land to raise their own poultry and they turned up their noses at shop-bought eggs and battery chickens.

The expert wives buying the birds drove a hard bargain: we could hear the odd derisory laugh at the mention of an initial asking price. When their customers had eventually selected their live purchases, the traders would swoop into the wire cages and pick the birds out, stuffing them into cardboard boxes with ready-made air-holes, for easy carriage home. We watched in admiration as the breeders picked up four grown chickens in one hand, holding them upside down by the feet while the fowl flapped their wings and protested loudly.

These stalls attracted the young children who stood mesmerised, fingers in mouths, studying the baby birds. As a special treat their grannies let them hold the cardboard boxes which they carried very carefully, often snatching a squint at the scrabbling occupants through the dark air-holes.

All the poultry traders were clustered around the steps of the town's Romanesque church. Take away the lorries and the plastic crates, we thought, and this scene must have been played out regularly since medieval times.

We turned back to the crossroads and walked towards the market square. An African trader's ethnic crafts looked strangely out of place against the stalls selling vegetable seedlings, bedding plants and geraniums. There were big stalls with striped awnings devoted just to strawberries or asparagus, set up by specialist growers, alongside folding tables displaying a few cheeses or some surplus plants offered by an enthusiastic amateur. This part of the market seemed to be zoned mainly for food and produce, though the odd hankie or handbag stall was mixed among them. We wondered how anyone could make a living selling hankies.

Hundreds of people milled about and it was hard to push a

way through occasional bottlenecks in the narrow street. Then it widened out into the area where the normal market was held twice a month and it was easier to browse around the stalls and the small funfair for children. We recognised some of the stalls, whose proprietors seemed to have negotiated to keep their usual pitches, especially the ones selling what we described as "pinnies" — the ubiquitous blue wrap-round pinafore or buttoned overall of the typical French country housewife. Scores of samples hung from bizarre wire frames which filled the shoulders and pushed out the fronts into angular shelf-like bosoms. When we'd first bought the house at St Paradis we had been unable to distinguish between our new female neighbours and we had invented the collective noun of "The Blue Pinnies" to describe them when seen from a distance. Now, of course, they were all old friends and valued as individuals. For sentimental reasons, I had always wanted a pinny but Jack refused to countenance it. He seemed to prefer me to do our DIY in my old working clothes. Perhaps he didn't want to be a Pinny's Husband.

The stalls spilled out of the market square and down all the roads which radiated from it. We had never seen so many in our lives. If the weather had been more cheerful it would have been impossible not to have been tempted to buy something, but the greyness and drizzle was putting a real damper on what should have been a carnival atmosphere. The choice of goods was enormous and what was on display in the peripheral streets was not the down-to-earth rural necessities of the other areas. You could buy tee-shirts, mini-skirts, bedlinen, trinkets, hats, shoes, cheap recordings, tatty kitchenware, fast food and even the work of a mason who carved statues to order.

It was too crowded for anyone to be able to put up an umbrella without it becoming an offensive weapon. We were damp and cold, interested in the spectacle but not in the mood to get the most out of it. As browsers buttoned their jackets and pulled up their coat collars, we sensed everyone else felt the same and were sorry for the traders who didn't seem to be selling much.

Suddenly we heard a siren and realised that an ambulance with flashing lights was trying to make its way through the dense crowd. People had to squash against the stalls and push between them in order to give it enough space to crawl past. At the next road junction, an excited little policeman blew away at his whistle and waved his arms importantly. He held back the people behind him so the ambulance could turn right. We couldn't tell whether there was a patient on board or if the medics were on their way to deal with an emergency. The vehicle was swallowed up in the throng and we didn't see it again.

We made for the horse market to see what was happening there. We found scores of horses and ponies of all descriptions tethered to metal railings, waiting for buyers to offer a price. They looked miserable, too, hunched up against the cold. The adjacent parking area was filled with horse-boxes and trailers. As horsy people, we were amused when, drawn by the unmistakable shrill squealing of equine passion, we saw a mare and stallion coupling in the midst of the crowds, watched laconically by their respective owners who had presumably arranged the match.

In a region where farm dogs work for their living, run miles every day and are never mollycoddled, we were equally amused and also mystified to see the number of pampered pooches being carried round in the arms of middle-aged women. Why bring a miniature poodle with bad breath and a jewelled collar to a horse sale, where it is likely to get kicked by an animal or trodden on by the crowds? We concluded these pets must belong to town people who had come a long distance to sample the fun of the fair rather than take part in a rural ritual. But why not leave the wretched dogs in their cars — or at home?

We decided to go and made our way back via the stalls associated with the horse trade — selling saddlery, tools, parts for trotting carts, string, rope, wellington boots and wooden clogs. Jack succumbed to temptation and bought some cheap tools and the odd pulley. We couldn't go home empty-handed.

At St Paradis we agreed that we hadn't really done justice to the famous horse fair. We'd go again another year when the sun was shining, and earlier in the day, too, before the crowds made it so claustrophobic.

The event had a knock-on effect for our hamlet for the rest of the day, as vehicles trying to avoid the blocked-off centre of the town made a detour past the house. We had more through traffic in a single afternoon than in a normal week.

After lunch we got on with putting a second coat of paint on the inside of the kitchen units so that the new chipboard backs were not obvious. Jack replaced the old-fashioned dim light-bulb in the back kitchen with a fluorescent light fitting, which illuminated the room properly for the first time. He discovered that the original light, installed presumably when electricity first came to the village, had been wired up backwards.

I wanted to continue the improvements I'd made at the end of the previous visit, when I had transformed the dirty grey and cream walls of the big kitchen by painting them brilliant white. We were determined to renovate the house but not change its character and I felt strongly that this should include not altering the basic colour scheme in the kitchen.

The room, 18ft x 18ft at its smallest, had doors leading off to the front, the old salon, the back kitchen, the staircase and the ground floor under-stairs area near the back door. These doors were all painted brown, as was the high wooden mantelpiece and a cupboard in the wall beside the fireplace. I'd bought some exterior grade brown paint in a sale which matched exactly, and I first tried it out on the cupboard door. This cupboard had always given me the creeps. It filled the depth of the granite wall and was lined with wood which had gone black over the years. In spite of being cleaned out it felt as though nameless things were lurking in the dark corners. From the beginning we'd decided we couldn't bring ourselves to put anything nice inside and it was now filled with DIY products and small tools. I decided to risk putting modern paint over the pre-war stuff. The door accepted the new brown gloss hungrily and it shone in a perfect glowing finish against the white emulsion. It looked so good I couldn't take my eyes off it. Full of enthusiasm, I painted the mantelpiece too until it gleamed in its smart new coat.

This success just reinforced our opinion that the house was taking part eagerly in its own restoration. It was like a pet at the vet's which submits patiently to the surgeon, knowing that skilled and sympathetic hands will make it better. We'd noticed from the very beginning that the jobs we tackled, though time-consuming, were not bedevilled by the Sod's Law complications which usually marred such a task at home. Even when Jack and our son Alex had replaced a rotten oak beam in the barn they had found another, exactly the right size, in the bread oven building.

The only thing that had gone wrong at St Paradis had been entirely my fault, when against my better judgment I had lazily painted white emulsion over powdery distemper on the spare bedroom ceiling and had to scrape it all off again.

We'd viewed the house quite by accident when an unexpected legacy had enabled us to hunt for a French property exactly two years before. It was out of our price range but we'd fallen in love at first sight in spite of the fact that it had been empty for years.

Our son Chris, who took part in the house-hunting, loved it too and lent us the money from his own legacy to enable us to buy it.

We were convinced the family had been drawn to St Paradis deliberately and that its late owner, the widow Marguerite, had somehow marked us down to inherit it. Her only son, Alain, to whom it should have passed, had died as a victim of the Nazis. He had been in the Resistance, had been caught and had been worked to death as a slave labourer. He had perished outside a Czechoslovakian concentration camp two days before VE-Day. He had been roughly the same age as Alex and Chris when he died and as a mother my heart had gone out to Marguerite in her terrible loss. Her spirit had filled the house in the early days and it seemed that she communicated with us by some sort of thought-transference through me. In the beginning she was constantly showing me the secrets of her beloved childhood home, but as time wore on the messages became more infrequent. It was as if she was quite content with what we were doing and could be at peace. Jack's only sadness was that she had never spoken to him.

*We opened the salon door for the first time in perhaps 50 years*

# Chapter Two – May 1996

The one job on the house which we did not contemplate doing ourselves was stripping the grimy green paint off the upstairs doors. They were very old and decorated with simple carving. We had never understood how they had become so filthy. We could see that busy farmers would want a working kitchen and might think that painting the bottom third of the walls grey was a way of disguising any muck which brushed off their boots or clothing. Yet two of the bedrooms had once been elegantly wallpapered, with pretty matching borders, and the others had been neatly painted — albeit a hundred years ago. Why should the doors, which had also originally been an attractive pale green, have ended up blackened and disfigured with dirt? Paul had suggested that it was years of being opened by men with smoking cigarettes between their fingers, and that theory would account for some of the filth. But the rest? We didn't know. We did know however that it had taken me half a day to clean a quarter of one door with steel wool, and that this was not a productive use of time. Michel's son had given us the address of a man in the nearest city who specialised in stripping doors and furniture and we had decided to ask him for a quote to do the four doors.

The original idea had been to telephone him. We both loathed speaking on the telephone in French, indeed you could say we were almost paranoid in our fear that the little black instrument of torture on the desk might require us to talk down it. We had only installed a telephone at St Paradis so that our family could keep in touch if there was a domestic emergency in England.

Jack was brushing up his French with weekly lessons at work, and he had been studying to take an Institute of Linguists' examination based on making a complicated telephone call. He had a good excuse for missing it — we had booked our holiday in France long before the examination date was announced but it clashed with our stay. We made a pact that I would be let off the trauma of telephoning the wood-stripping man and Jack could do it as a penance for missing his exam. He had even practised what to say.

When we went to the city next day to do some shopping, Jack decided to look out for the stripping place "so that we will know where to bring the doors." The address sounded simple on paper but we discovered that the name of what we took to be a suburb was very loose and the actual premises were miles away. When we eventually found them, he parked outside and said casually: "I think we ought to check out the quality of the guy's workmanship. We can't have him ruining those beautiful doors with harsh chemicals."

So he went into the workshop, inspected some nicely-stripped doors, introduced himself to the man and asked him for a quote. Face to face.

The man was very easy to understand. We chatted. We talked about our doors, his business, his long working hours and his dog which was recovering from being run over. We discussed how he lived in a caravan in a corner of the industrial unit so he didn't have to go home when he was busy. We told him the long story of our house renovations. We agreed a price and said we'd bring the doors in our trailer the following day. He said he would try to do them by the weekend.

The telephone rang and he disappeared into his little office to answer it.

"You crook!" I said to Jack. "You've broken your bargain and deliberately flunked your exam. We've been discussing for weeks about how you would speak to him on the phone…"

"Oh dear…" said Jack, innocently. "So we have. What a shame!"

Back home we became engrossed in putting decorative beading round the door frame leading from the kitchen into the back kitchen and making shelves for the larder unit. We lost track of time and discovered that we were eating a quick lunch at 4pm — sacrilege in a country where everything stops between noon and 2pm so that people can enjoy their food in a civilised fashion.

We put primer on the beading, which replaced the original carved decoration that had been eaten by woodworm. Before we took it off, little piles of wood dust would shake out of the frame whenever the door banged. Other parts of the house suffered superficially from woodworm, but this was the worst infestation.

Then we donned our anoraks, scarves and boots, and went to "beat the bounds" round the two-acre field at the back. It was still ridiculously cold for May and our unworn summer clothes were hanging neglected in the wardrobe.

First we looked in the newly-discovered outhouse for the wooden wheelbarrow that Paul had described. It had been painted blue and was massive. We were full of respect for any Limousin farmer who could have pushed it empty, let alone with a full load. It looked as if it had been made by the same craftsman who made the local farm carts and to a very similar design. However, wheelbarrows were always useful and we were pleased to have such a good relic of the farm's working days. It stood in a part of the building behind and at the side of the henhouse where we had found a plastic egg during our first stay at St Paradis. There were wire cages in rows at the back, which we supposed might have been for rabbits. The hens had been free-range and had entered their henhouse via a presumably fox-proof hole in the stone wall.

Our curiosity satisfied, we started to explore the field. We only had about a quarter of an acre in Hartford so it was fun to contemplate and manage our much larger domain in France. It stretched out behind the house, the land dropping quite steeply to the right. There had once been a stone wall around two sides, but it had fallen into disrepair and had been reinforced by a hedge which now ran all the way round. The part of the field which continued along the line of the house frontage bordered the main street of St Paradis. There was a ten-foot gateway between our pigsties and the remains of the wall and nearby our deep well was covered by a wooden frame to stop children and wildlife falling in. Both the well and the pigsties were overshadowed by a horse chestnut tree which was covered in cream "candles" at this time of year. The base of the trunk and its roots were protected by big boulders.

Down the left-hand side was a grassy pathway which was cut periodically by the commune's handyman. Alongside, on our land, there had once been a *lavoir* or public pool where the village women did their laundry. It was now silted up and full of fallen trees but you could still discern the stone blocks which had surrounded the edges. One day we intended to excavate it and restore it to its former state. A little stream fed into it and the constant water supply into a blocked-up pond made that part of the field very boggy. When our friend Georges, the agricultural contractor, cut the hay we could see from the deep tyre tracks which remained afterwards that he always got stuck trying to snatch the last stalks of grass in that area.

Where the grassy path met the tiny road which ran parallel to the bottom of the field, there was a pond occupied by Mme Echelle's ducks — and lots of frogs. We used to catch the *grenouilles* by surprise and watch them diving into the deep end, doing a spectacular breast-stroke out of sight. During the day we could hear the quacking conversation of the ducks and at night there was a chorus of croaking frogs.

The right-hand border of the field zig-zagged in a strange way to accommodate a small field which seemed to have been arbitrarily cut out of one corner. We assumed that it had been done as part of the division of land under a will in the distant past. The terrain dropped down into a corner where, in wet weather, there was the trill of a tiny waterfall. At this point it met a pathway which made a forked join with another bigger one that ran down the right-hand side of the house and eventually led to a nearby hamlet. In the summer our path was so overgrown as to be almost impassable but the other was kept open by tractors forcing their way down to otherwise inaccessible fields.

We traipsed down to the bottom of the field to have a look at four oak saplings which we'd had planted a year before. They'd been over two feet high when we put them in and then they had either been eaten or rolled on by a big bull and his family which had taken over the field a few days later. The cattle had disdained our wooden stakes and anti-rabbit wire cages and had reduced the oaks to nine-inch twigs. Twelve months on, we were pleased to see that they had recovered but they were still comparatively tiny. We wanted them to grow up and hide an ugly concrete electricity sub-station which dominated that part of the view from the house but it looked as if our heirs would have to wait to see that happen. We suspected that at this rate, the oaks would probably still be twigs when we were pushing up the daisies.

It was 10pm when we finally had our supper, listening to Dire Straits tapes which we had brought from home.

The following morning we filled the gaps and hollows in the back kitchen door with ready-mixed filler. We struggled downstairs with the four doors, which reminded me that my battered ribs were far from better, and tied them down in the trailer ready for the trip to the stripping company after lunch.

When we came back from the city we cleared out the old salon enough to construct a set of big Dexion shelves. We were fed up with having tools and equipment strewn at random all over the floor and wanted to tidy them up. Making the salon into a respectable workshop — which was all it had ever been used for by the previous owners — was one of our goals on this holiday.

Between ourselves we had always called the room the *atelier* (workshop) although it formed an integral part of the house. It had a beamed ceiling, an unused fireplace and rotten oak floorboards. The walls had been plastered but not painted and the plaster was falling away in many places. The room was 12ft 10ins wide and 26ft 6ins long, running from the front to the back of the house, with a normal narrow window at the back. To the right of the window was a cupboard with sagging door, that appeared to have been made out of a doorway which had led out the back before the stairs were built.

To the left of the window we had been led one day by Marguerite to discover where she had written her name in pencil on the walls at various ages. The lowest was in big, babyish capital letters, scrunching up as she ran out of space. A little above, she had written her name again, in childish script. Further up, the writing was more grown-up and laboriously joined-up. Then on the wall at right angles, in grown-up flowing writing, she had signed her name with a flourish and added her address underneath. We had been thrilled to find these signs of her life there and had vowed that whenever we modernised the room we would find a way of preserving them. Sadly, they were now fading rapidly, as though they had served their purpose by being found.

At the front was an interesting door, with solid wood at the bottom and a window at the top which had a wooden shutter bolted over it to make it burglar-proof. We had hung a net curtain over the glass, so that prying eyes could not see what was stored in the room, and usually took the shutter off when we were in residence to make the place lighter. It had very little natural light and was grey and gloomy. We doubted if this front door had been opened for at least 50 years.

Six feet into the room from the door was a trapdoor leading down to the cellar, and to the left was a clearly defined doorway which had once led directly into the barn but was now blocked up with unplastered stones.

We'd had the impression from the start that the room had been built as a salon when the house was extended in the 19th century (perhaps because the extra bedrooms were required above it), but that social life had continued to revolve around the spacious kitchen and the posh new dining room had never been finished. From that point it had degenerated into a junkroom and place to do odd jobs.

We knew that the cellar had been used for storing cheeses from the St Paradis dairy because one of the old women in the village told us she used to carry them down there as a child, and had been frightened of the dark.

Making the Dexion shelves, it took ages to get the bolts in the right holes and to manhandle everything into position. By this time I knew that sore ribs were not terminal and just put up with the discomfort. I was encouraged to do this because, by siting the Dexion where we needed it, we were reluctantly — but temporarily — covering up the one reference to Marguerite's son which remained in the house. Years before, probably as a young teenager copying his mother's example, Alain had written his name in pencil on the bare plaster. I could only guess at what he had subsequently suffered and did not have the cheek to complain about my own minor twinges.

Next morning, Wednesday, Vivienne, one of my French "cousins" (the children of my mother's best friend) telephoned and arranged to come to stay for several days the following week. This gave us an incentive to get even more jobs completed before she and her husband Jacques arrived. We were proud of St Paradis and dearly wanted everyone else to love it too — especially French people.

On our second visit to the house we had covered the bare concrete floor in the kitchen with second-hand hard-wearing carpet tiles, which made the room warmer as well as more cheerful. We now put the remainder down in the back kitchen, which had an immediately homely effect.

Our Dutch friends Beatrice and Jan dropped by and invited us over for a meal on Sunday evening. Then a young man who said he was with the travelling chimney sweep knocked on the door and offered their services. We thought it was about time the chimney in the kitchen was swept, as we had already scraped a lot of tarry residues out of it ourselves, and agreed that they should come back on Friday.

We took the door off the back kitchen so we could plane a little from the bottom to make it go over the carpet tiles and discovered it was a lot more badly affected with woodworm than we had realised. Jack exhibited all his qualities of scientific patience by injecting every single hole with a cow syringe full of woodworm treatment. We had bought it at our vet's in Cheshire for just such an eventuality. However we hadn't reckoned on treating 80 separate holes! It was fascinating to follow the course of the liquid as it squirted through the eaten-out channels and appeared somewhere quite unexpected.

Then we made a quick trip to the *départemental* capital to pay our Travellers Cheques into our bank account. We had learned by trial and error that this was the most efficient method of transferring money from England to France. We stocked up with food from the big hypermarket, and did the rounds of the DIY places looking for concrete slabs to make a solid surface outside the salon door.

Back home we bumped into Michel and remarked on the miserable weather. He said it would carry on like this for some time and quoted some local folklore to back up his assertion. We had no doubt that he would be right — he usually was.

Thursday, May 16 was Ascension Day, a bank holiday in

France. It was a day to pay family visits and we saw lots of our friends who had popped over to St Paradis to call on their relatives. We didn't see Paul. He had gone off on holiday to Brittany with an old friend. For the first time, the weather was actually nice.

We spent the entire day working on the salon. We stacked a good amount of plumbing, electrical and woodworking tools in boxes on the Dexion shelves, together with dozens of cans of paint, varnish and magic liquids that did everything from cleaning paintbrushes to waterproofing walls. Rolls of cable, ducting, flex and wire went up there too and we attached 4m lengths of copper pipe to the top deck. A blue hard hat was the crowning glory.

We brushed the floor thoroughly and hoovered up the dust and flakes of wood which were constantly coming off the disintegrating oak floorboards. We noted the most spongy and broken boards and marked them out for replacement.

We couldn't bring ourselves to throw away two large boxes of "empties" which dated back to the turn of the century. Some had labels in almost mint condition. Marguerite's family, the Xaviers, had been hoarders and we had museum pieces on our hands from all over the house. Paul was less sentimental. Every time he saw the old bottles, which had contained mineral waters, spirits and tonic wine, he said: "You know where the bottle bank is, don't you?"

In the salon we'd also "inherited" a couple of home-made benches which we had been told had been used for festivities like harvest suppers, when the Xaviers would have entertained their friends and family. The benches were made from tree trunks sawn in half, with crude legs inserted into the curved side at each end and in the middle. We doubted if they had been very stable, but they would have seated around ten people each. We also had some in the attic. We carried them out and put them in the barn.

We also had a spare front door. Out of interest we measured it and found it wouldn't fit anywhere in our house. We wondered if it had belonged to an old burnt-out house opposite which we had unwittingly bought with the rest of the property. It had belonged to Marguerite but had burned down in the 1980s. All we had been left with was a roofless eyesore with a dangerous cellar. We had sold it to our neighbour, M. Lebrun, whose second home abutted it, for 200FF. (The *notaire* wouldn't allow a smaller sum!). He planned to knock it down and create an attractive garden on the site, and we felt this would be far more beneficial to the village than anything we could do with it. We could hardly afford to renovate our own house, without having to spend money making another one safe. As far as we were concerned, it was a liability.

The day's most exciting project was to open the salon's front door. We brushed all the cobwebs away and cleaned around it thoroughly. It was fortified like Alcatraz. We oiled the lock so that the ancient key would turn and we applied WD40 to the bolts until they would slide. Then we assaulted the hinges with WD40. With Jack pulling and me pushing from the outside, it eventually gave way with a groan. We worked it an inch or two at a time until it was fully open and daylight streamed into the room for the first time since the war — or probably before. We had a great sense of achievement. The house was yielding up its last dark places and basking in the unaccustomed sunshine. The once spooky room assumed an entirely new character.

Jack celebrated by starting a bonfire to get rid of the rubbish we'd cleared out. I've always thought he was a budding pyromaniac.

Next morning the telephone rang. We were unconcerned, thinking it would be my cousin with a change of plan. I was nearest and I answered it.

"*Bonjour Madame,*" said the door stripping man. "*Vos portes sont finis...*"

I panicked then collected myself while he told me he had worked on the doors all over the bank holiday so that they would be finished early for us. They were lovely wood, poplar and pear, and he was very pleased with them. We could collect them any time.

I was very miffed that Jack hadn't even had a minute on the phone with him.

Jack continued to feed the bonfire. He cut the down the remaining ivy on the wall in the back garden and burnt it, pleased that the smoke was blowing away from our house and directly into the empty grounds of the Lebruns, who were usually only in residence during the summer. When the fire was at its smokiest, we were horrified to see a car being driven past our kitchen window and straight into the Lebruns' drive. We hoped the occupants stayed indoors.

Then the sweep arrived with his assistant. He was a real wide boy and we took an instant dislike to him. He obviously saw us as easy prey.

First he disputed the quote the lad had given us.

"The boy never said the chimney was as big as this," he grumbled. "I'll have to charge you extra."

We argued that was his problem. The assistant had been quite capable of seeing that we had a vast *cantou* and not a little domestic chimney.

They set out their groundsheets and attacked the chimney with a scraper. Very little soot came down — a tiny amount in comparison with the sacksful we had dislodged ourselves the year before. We must have made a very thorough job of it.

The sweep gave us a certificate to say he'd swept the kitchen chimney and then asked what other fireplaces there were in the house. We knew none of them had been used for generations and we certainly had no intention of lighting fires in them ourselves. We admitted to having a fireplace in the salon (he had seen the chimney!) but explained that it had never been used. The plaster inside was still white and the firebricks were virginal. He said our insurance wouldn't be valid if we didn't have a certificate for it. He'd give us one for 100F. What if there was a fire and it could be traced back to having started in this chimney? It was only sensible to cover ourselves, he said. We indicated that we were willing to take such a multi-million to one chance. Then increasingly less politely we told him to get lost and he eventually went away, shaking his head at our profligacy.

We went to the city and collected the stripped doors. They were beautiful. We could now see the original marks made by the carpenter's tools over 100 years before.

We then bought the only concrete slabs we could find anywhere which were the right sandy colour. We only wanted four but we had decided to experiment with how they weathered and, if we were satisfied, to use similar ones for the terrace at the back when we got round to it.

Home at St Paradis it rained and we had our first thunder-storm of the visit. The house is in an area bounded by two high voltage power lines, each about five kilometres away, and Michel told us long ago that they usually deflect thunderstorms but if a storm crosses into this channel, it will be very violent. We had seen ample evidence of this in the past.

We chatted with Hugo and his wife who said they were inter-ested in buying a house in the district. They had vaguely looked at one in the village. It belonged to M Lebrun but appeared to be part of Michel's farmyard. The property was strange: it consisted of a rather handsome little house which had been empty for very many years, a paved area and a stone farm building on two floors opposite. And that was all. There was no other land. The house could be modernised. The outbuilding could be turned into a garage with a loft. But nothing could be done about the lack of space. Should you wish to stand on the paving and swing a cat, it would probably bump its nose on the walls. The house was also up on a high bank, so the only access was via the farmyard. We all agreed that it was a great shame. It seemed as if the property was likely to remain empty for ever. In a region full of deserted and handsome old houses, it had very little going for it.

Today, Saturday, it alternated between beautiful weather, thun-derstorms and torrential rain. Unfortunately I had done the wash-ing during a deceptively nice period and every time I hung it out on the line to dry it got rained on. I used the opportunity to cam-paign very vociferously for a tumble-drier. In the evening we hung it round the log fire and added in a fan heater for good mea-sure.

Earlier I coated the study ceiling with stabiliser to prime the dusty pink distemper which had been painted on it between the wars — or even earlier. It was my most detested job, as the stuff was very runny and very sticky and persisted in dripping down my arm from the bristles of the brush. It was like painting with watery treacle. The liquid also attacked ordinary rubber gloves and made them pucker up. It was the job I had been hoping to avoid the previous year when I painted modern emulsion straight on to the spare bedroom ceiling, and I had learned to my cost that I couldn't get away with it.

Meanwhile, Jack started to mend the floor in the salon, using his router to cut out the most badly damaged parts of the floorboards so that he could replace them. We had found a good store of seasoned oak planks leaning in a tepee-like shape against one of the walls of the salon when we took over the house. A receipt dated 1923 had fallen out when I moved the wood.

During his excavations, Jack worked out why the floor had gone so rotten. The wide hand-cut oak floorboards had been laid on wooden joists which rested on the rock and over the years gaps had opened up between them. Through these gaps had fallen — or more likely been brushed by conscientious farmers' wives — enough mud and dust to fill up the spaces between the joists and prevent the wood from "breathing."

We knew we would have to replace the floor some time but just at the moment we thought it would be nice to walk on it without getting a sinking feeling.

By way of light relief we drove to another major town, south of St Paradis, where we sussed out a new *bricolage* and found a new food supermarket. We'd always been snooty about the Stoc chain before, thinking it was pretty downmarket, but we admitted we had been mistaken. We were impressed and agreed in future to patronise another branch nearer home.

That night Jack brought St Paradis into the 20th century by setting up an old computer on the kitchen table. As a professional computing expert, he suffered from withdrawal symptoms if he did not have a machine at hand. We were going to use it to write a checklist for visitors to the house, while we could actually see what was necessary, then take the information home on disk and print it out into a little guidebook.

The next day we were both very busy again. I painted the first coat of brilliant white emulsion on the study ceiling and then painted the walls peach. Next I put white undercoat on the door frames. They were not attractive enough to strip down to the bare wood and the white would provide a contrast with the plain wood of the newly treated doors. We couldn't varnish these yet as they had not dried out. That would have to wait for another holiday. Michel's son, who had originally recommended the stripping firm, came to have a look and was pleased with the result. It was obvious that the man had used gentle chemicals and a lot of care.

Jack was busy replacing the floorboards. The "new" oak was conspicuous by its cleanliness. Then he installed the computer on a special metal stand in the corner of the kitchen. It looked rather incongruous beside the ancient smoke-blackened fireplace.

Just in time we managed to get clean and tidy ready to go off to Beatrice and Jan for supper. We enjoyed a happy evening with them and their two French Spaniels, who looked like a cross between a Pointer and a Setter and were always delightful. For us it was a luxury to speak English socially, and Beatrice said it was for her, too. English was much closer to Dutch than French, she said, and it was so nice not to have to remember the gender of the words. Why should a lamp-post be described as masculine or feminine? This reminded me of the time when Jack — slightly tongue in cheek, but quite serious — told a French evening class teacher: "My French vocabulary is OK but I do have such trouble with sex..."

She looked nonplussed then laughed and corrected him.

"Gender!" she said. "You mean gender..."

*The little Bishop's statue had the proportions of a child's body*

# Chapter Three – May 1996

W̶e owe a debt of gratitude to Stoc for helping us to find our favourite drive in the world. It happened like this.

When we mentioned our newly-discovered supermarket to the neighbours they laughed and said that practically everyone in the area shopped at the local branch ten kilometres away.

"Fancy you not knowing that!" they exclaimed. "Why, you can go there at any time of day and bump into someone you know."

We knew the way by the main roads, but Jack decided to try a shorter cross-country route which he had worked out from the map. We much preferred to travel like this, drinking in the real *France Profonde*.

The lanes were narrow and winding, often with steep banks covered in wild flowers. Groups of cattle grazed lazily in the meadows: the cows giving their calves a quick suckle while the bulls looked on protectively. Hamlets as tiny as ours cropped up every kilometre or so. They too had dogs lying in the centre of the road which shifted out of the way resentfully when they saw a strange car. Tractors chugged around, towing well-used and muddy implements, masters of the meandering lanes.

The granite houses, as always in this region, were wellbuilt and classical in their simplicity. Window-ledges, doorways and garden paths were vibrant with pot plants and the front doors were mostly open, inviting a fleeting peep into their dark interiors. Several were empty, their drooping shutters revealing grimy broken windows. Some of these sad houses had simply been absorbed into the farm buildings — a peasant family's former dwelling now given over to storing fertiliser and tools. Others seemed to have been abandoned.

Romanesque churches stood proudly in the centre of the larger hamlets, probably now, like the one at St Paradis, only used for funerals. Gently arched stone bridges crossed small streams. Occasionally we could see an *etang* (pool) which someone had created for fishing.

There was so little traffic that outside one farm we were nearly lifted off our wheels by a young woman driving a tractor with a front loader for spearing giant bales of hay. She had driven straight out of the gate without looking, as she obviously always did. She grinned apologetically and we waved back. It was her road, not ours.

Over the years we've made it our road, too. We love every inch of it. It changes with the weather and the seasons and it's always enchanting.

We found the Stoc and bought the food we needed for entertaining Vivienne and Jacques over the following couple of days. I was disappointed that there wasn't a selection of pre-packed ready-priced meat. This meant I had to work out what I wanted from first principles and ask for it on the butchery counter. It was almost as much of an ordeal as using the telephone. Just how big is a kilo of *jarret*? What the heck do you do with it when you've got it? What's the difference between *gigot* and *gilet*? French meat is cut differently from ours and I'd had some culinary disasters in the past when I'd used inappropriate cooking methods. The English equivalent, I suppose, would be trying to roast a hunk of tough shin stewing beef.

It hailed on the way back to St Paradis: we really were being very unlucky with the weather.

Fired up to do as much as possible before our guests arrived, I painted a second coat of white on the study ceiling, put the finishing touches to the peach walls and went over the skirting boards and door frames with white gloss where they needed it. Then I put white emulsion on the part of the landing which led into the study — it was currently an unappetising and dirty green. This marked where the massive stone wall of the original house had been broken through when it was extended to include the salon, the study and the spare bedroom.

Jack renewed the wires supporting the big vine across the front of the house and retrained the branches, pruning some off. He put wiring for power and light in flexible plastic conduits running through the salon wall into the barn, fitted the conduit to the salon's beamed ceiling and insulated the nearby water pipes which came through from the stopcock in the barn. Then he wired up new lights and a power socket in the barn so he could use his woodworking machinery out there.

We went to bed eventually — shattered but quite pleased with ourselves.

While we waited for Vivienne and Jacques to arrive next morning, we put up the candelabra-type light fitting we'd bought for the study. We were disappointed to find that the bulbs we had got didn't fit and we broke one by trying to force it into the holder. We dismantled the light so we could put in a single 100watt bulb for our guests' convenience and broke one of the glass shades when we replaced it in its box.

When my cousins arrived they admired the house and we talked non-stop for hours. I had prepared a roast chicken for our evening meal but was so engrossed in family gossip that I failed to notice that the bottled gas for the cooker had run out almost immediately after I had lit it. When I went to put on the vegetables, the burners were dead and the meat in the oven was almost raw. Dinner was delayed by an hour and a half and I was devastated.

However, the pleasure of being in one another's company made up for the setbacks. I was particularly touched by Vivienne's deep affection for my mother, who is her godmother. She told us how Mother had thought constantly about her "French family" during the war, when they were unable to communicate, and how Mother had faithfully put aside money for Vivienne each birthday and Christmas until she had saved enough to buy her a new bicycle when the war was over.

Vivienne, who has excellent taste in expensive French clothes, takes the same size as me. She's in her sixties but dresses well and casually. By a very welcome tradition we've established, she brought me a bulging goody bag of clothes she no longer wanted to wear (perhaps the French equivalent of a food parcel) and they fitted perfectly. I am wearing one of her blouses as I write this. She gave it to me eight years ago and it's still as good as new.

The following morning I went through Vivienne's collection and put on a pair of culottes and a snazzy polo shirt. We all wandered round exploring the village, pleased that the weather had brightened enough for jackets not to be necessary. Mme Echelle was tending her animals and we stopped for a chat. Her menagerie included two pregnant goats, various rabbits, free-range chickens and geese, several ducks on the pond, her dogs Gitane and Soupette, and a white cat. Seven hunting dogs in a kennel in the back garden belonged to one of her sons. Her house is the old *auberge* opposite the church and she is custodian of the keys. We were delighted when she offered to open it up for us, for we had never been inside. Michel had once told us that when he was a child he had heard tell of the *curé* who had painted the interior with a palette knife but we did not know what to expect and we couldn't really date when the work had been done. We concluded it must have been late in the 1800s.

When our eyes became accustomed to the dim light, an extraordinary sight awaited us. Every inch of the walls had been covered with stencilled designs. In the main body of the church they were on a white background and in the lady chapel they were on blue. Each little pattern contained several colours intricately running into one another. Archways and windows were picked out with their own elaborate designs. Simply making the templates to fit must have been a highly-skilled job.

The ceiling was wooden and curved like a barrel. Its decoration was in two distinct halves. The back section was a continuation of the stencilling with red and blue flowers and motifs on a white background. It seemed bright and fresh in comparison with the front part, which looked very much older and moved me enormously. In painted golden "picture frames", fading with age and surrounded by a veritable jungle of blue acanthus leaves, were several separate figures: Christ, Our Lady, the saintly bishop after whom the church had been named, and some other holy characters whom I couldn't identify.

Our Lady was the pretty standard rendition — a pious young woman with a halo, white veil, blue cloak and red dress. She had her hands clasped and was gazing up to heaven past her eyelashes in a pose made famous in hundreds of photographs of Princess Diana.

The bishop was altogether more worldly. Under his white mitre he had a chubby face with pink cheeks, full lips and protruding eyes. He wore a richly decorated blue cope edged with gold and looked more like a 20-year-old theological student with doubts about his vocation than a saint.

The Christ figure was the most amazing. I presumed he was Jesus because he looked too young to be God the Father although he was posed against a blue sky and fluffy grey clouds. Perhaps he had just ascended into Heaven. He had a golden halo, long brown hair tending to a thinness on top and a luxuriant brown beard which spilled onto his chest. His skin was smooth and his eyes were large and clear. He wore a white long-sleeved garment with gold trimmings and a white belt tucked up almost under his armpits. His right hand was raised in benediction and over his left arm he carried a red cloak. But what really made me stop in my tracks was the fact that in his left hand he held a carefully painted *blue hat*!

Now I'm no student of the history of art but I was brought up as a Catholic and I've seen my share of devotional statues and pictures in all extremes of good and bad taste. I am quite sure that I have never seen a painting of Christ with a hat before. I don't know why not — perhaps it would have got in the way of his halo? This hat was no Middle-Eastern headgear; it was round, with a brim, and I could imagine it being worn by a Frenchman long ago.

I couldn't take my eyes off the pictures as I tried to discern all the details in the dim light. The painting of the Virgin Mary was pretty characterless but the other two were fascinating. Looked at dispassionately, they were quite crudely executed — for this was no Sistine Chapel. But that was their charm. They looked as though they had been painted by a local man several hundred years before, probably in conditions of considerable discomfort, using a limited palette of colours and an unpromising canvas of oak planks. The nails holding the boards in place had gone rusty and the ceiling was dotted with black nail-heads which spoilt the detail of his handiwork. Had the ceiling originally been plain? How long ago had the tiny community scrimped and saved to raise the funds and pay the artist to honour their patron saint, Jesus and his Mother? I doubted if anyone had the answers now.

The altar was backed by a massive wooden screen which took up the end wall of the church. It was ornately carved, with a layer of grey dust on the carvings. At the top was a statue of a bearded figure — Christ, John the Baptist? — wearing what appeared to be a gold loincloth with gold material draped artistically over one arm. In the other hand he held a slightly bent staff. At his feet was a white object. The figure stood on a little plinth and was so high up that it was impossible to see what this object was. It came to just below his knee-height and might have been a wine pitcher or something inanimate but it looked awfully like a small lamb or a dog gazing upwards at its master. I hoped it was.

In niches on either side of the altar were almost identical statues of the bishop. It was hard to tell at a distance whether they were painted wood or plaster, but once again they looked very old. He was holding a crozier and wearing a red and gold cope lined with blue over a white over-garment and a black cassock which reached to the ground. His face was striking — with bright pink cheeks, full lips and big eyes — and was almost childlike on the left-hand statue, which was also modelled in childlike bodily proportions. Under the niches, supporting the bases on their wings, were two angels with wide, fat faces and black curly hair. One looked like a doll and the other's expression reminded me of Mrs Thatcher. In front of each was a little table covered with a white cloth bearing two candlesticks and a glass vase full of plastic roses.

There were plastic flowers everywhere in what we supposed was a valiant attempt to keep up appearances and give the impression of a building which was still in use and dedicated to the worship of God. But the tabernacle on the old high altar was empty and no light burned to show the presence of the consecrated Host. The soul had gone from the church but its body remained.

The stained glass windows were conventional and colourful, depicting the Bishop, St Paul, St Peter, St John the Baptist and the Sacred Heart. One was an abstract pattern. I didn't know if this showed the taste of the donor or the age of the window.

Familiar names covered the black marble memorial to the dead and missing of the First World War who had come from the parish. There were no Xaviers — their menfolk must have been among the lucky ones who survived. Next to it was an intricately carved wooden structure displaying a simple statue of a grieving Virgin Mary with the body of Christ lying across her knees. She was surprisingly buxom and he was thin and small. It was disconcerting.

Looking around the church it was plain to see that there were two "schools" of statuary. The first were these old ones, which, while perhaps naively done, were full of vigour. The others were the standard plaster painted saints that presumably helped with the congregation's devotions but which were mass-produced and could be found in churches everywhere. I much preferred the former.

Rows of simple wooden pews, seating three or four people, filled the church on either side of the aisle. The floor was stone, discoloured by damp. A wooden pulpit topped by a carved canopy was reached by wooden steps, and pictures showing the Stations of the Cross hung at intervals round the walls. A new altar had been placed facing the congregation — presumably when such things were decreed under the reforms of the 1960s. It was covered with an embroidered cloth, two candlesticks, two vases and a metal cross.

We went up into the gallery by a twisting wooden staircase. Mouse droppings were pretty much in evidence here. The walls of the staircase had their own simple stencil design of crosses, lines and dots, while the gallery itself, which overlooked the body of the church, was picked out in pink leaves. Ropes hung through holes in the ceiling ready for the bells in the tower above to be tolled at the next funeral. There was a stained glass window depicting St Peter's papal headgear and the keys of heaven, bordered by a glorious fernlike stencil which, like all the others, fitted exactly.

My attempts at decorative stencilling have been a dismal failure but I am the family wallpaperer and I could only guess at the complexity of the task undertaken by the *curé* when he worked out and executed his lovely designs. It must have taken him many years. It was so sad to think that his unique church was rarely visited nowadays. Even in the big church in the nearby town, Masses were only said once a month or so. Little country churches like this were doomed to deteriorate through lack of use and maintenance, their congregations having dwindled away. We wished there was something we could do to save it. It reminded us of our precious farmhouse, which had called to us when we viewed it: "I'm dirty and neglected now but I used to be elegant and loved. Please restore my dignity!"

We took Vivienne and Jacques to the city that afternoon and explored the medieval quarter. To our shame we knew the city's supermarkets and *bricolages* but we hadn't ventured into the ancient centre. It was well worth it.

They left the following morning and I spent the day putting the finishing touches to the decorations in the study — painting the gloss surfaces and running a frieze round the top of the walls which echoed the design in the curtains from two kingsize patterned sheets. I had bought them at Northwich Market for £5 each nearly two years earlier from our favourite linen mill trader. He told me they had sold for £25 each in the shops and I'd subsequently found them at that price in various department stores. They had been lying made-up in a trunk in our bedroom at St Paradis for 18 months waiting for us to get round to doing the study.

While I was busy with the decorating, Jack strimmed the top of the field and the back garden and rebuilt a dry stone wall near the well, where the stones from the original wall had been lying in a disorganised heap for years.

That evening I finally managed to persuade him to stop working and relax. After all, that's what you're supposed to do on holiday! We put two green plastic chairs out in the back garden, opened a bottle of wine and balanced the glasses on the rather uneven surface of the granite steps up to the back door. It felt quite decadent to be sitting together in the golden rays of the setting sun... In fact, it was so unusual to see Jack sitting down that I took a couple of photographs to immortalise the occasion. I'm afraid I manage to enjoy quite a lot of little rests with a *peu de rouge*, but then I'm not a workaholic!

Next morning we drove to the town to buy some bread and stopped off on the way home at the village cemetery to pay our respects to Marguerite. We tried to do this during every visit to St Paradis. The photographs of her mother, husband and son which are displayed on the grave were incredibly clear and I took some photographs of them in case the light was better than in the previous ones I'd taken.

I mentioned to Jack that I was sorry she hadn't "talked" to me this time at all.

He replied: "I know it sounds stupid, but I think she might be trying to get in touch with me. I've been having the most peculiar things happening to my power tools. You know how careful I am with them. Obviously you have to switch them off before you turn them off at the mains and take out the plug. Well, for the past few days, I've switched things on at the mains and they've started on their own. I had the belt sander shoot off across the workbench and onto the floor. It was actually locked 'on' — and you can't put it down like that. I can't have left it on. It's happened with the electric drill and other things too — made me jump out of my skin. I've been using these tools for years and never known anything like it. It's as though someone is playing a game with me or trying to attract my attention."

Back home we cursed as we tried to put up a wooden curtain rail in the study. With walls made of stone you can't win. You either get a hernia drilling into solid granite or else you mistakenly pick a place which is soft mortar and the plastic wallplugs won't hold. We ended up with a near-hernia on one side of the rail and a hole full of Polyfilla on the other.

We just managed to finish the gloss paint and tidy up by the time Michel and his wife came for a drink before lunch. We were going to their home for a reciprocal *aperitif* the following day.

The couple were our source of knowledge about the village. This time they told us that the burned house which we had sold to the Lebruns had been hit by lightning during a thunderstorm. The roof had caught fire, a carpenter's workshop in the building had fuelled the flames and the interior of the house had literally dissolved away over time because the inside walls had been of *pisé* (clay). We had always wondered about what seemed a strange set of levels and steps and Michel explained that what appeared to be the ground floor of the remains was in fact the *sous-sol*. The ground floor had been reached by steps which at one time we had taken for a kind of mounting-block — which explained why the old *cantou* fireplace appeared to be half-way up one wall. He said that the cellar was in the corner and this confirmed our fears that Paul might have fallen down the hole while he was kindly trying to clear out the vegetation in the shell for us. We were glad we had sold the building and were no longer responsible for it.

We told them we had been in the church and Michel said that the day before had been the feast day of the village's namesake. It seemed an extraordinary coincidence that we should have explored it on the eve of the saint's day. Michel told us how until about 30 years ago, it was always marked by an annual festival in the village with a Mass and a procession when a statue of the saint was carried round to all the significant spots — the wells and the Calvaries — on the men's shoulders. This was followed by a celebration at the *auberge* and a dance in the public room upstairs. He was very sad that this no longer happened and that yet another village tradition had fallen by the wayside.

We mentioned that we'd seen a horse in the field by his farmhouse and he said he was very happy to have it as a lodger. He'd worked with oxen, horses and tractors during his lifetime as a farmer and he liked the horses best.

We thought: "What changes he's seen in St Paradis!" How tragic that in one or two generations it had gone from a thriving self-sufficient community to one where most of the inhabitants were over 60 and a good proportion of the houses were either standing empty or used as second homes.

That afternoon I painted everything brown I could lay my brush on in the kitchen until I ran out of paint. The gloss made an enormous difference to the feel of the place. It was still essentially the same — Marguerite would have recognised it all — but so much fresher. While we were working we had our usual daily visitors: Betty, the little brown dog who lived a couple of doors away with her shy elderly missus, and Gitane, who was always delighted to wriggle her way into the kitchen for a cuddle and a biscuit.

On our last full day at St Paradis during this holiday, we got up as usual. Since we had no bathroom and no running hot water, our routine was that Jack got out of bed first and went downstairs to the loo. Then he'd put the kettle and a large saucepan of water on the gas cooker to heat up, and use it to wash and shave at the kitchen sink. What was left was used to make coffee for breakfast. When I judged that the water temperature was about right, I would go down to the loo and then bring up a jug of hot water. I'd pour it into a bowl standing on a Victorian chest of drawers in our bedroom, and do my own ablutions. When I'd washed and dressed I would take the bowl of water downstairs and throw it on the flowerbed.

This morning was no different. I went downstairs and found Jack looking very puzzled and a bit shaken.

"I think I might have seen Marguerite," he said. "Of course it's much more possible that it was something odd happening with my bifocals. But I was standing here at the sink and I thought I heard someone come downstairs. Naturally, I thought it was you. I turned round and saw a person in light-coloured long clothes — which I took to be you in your long dressing gown — go from the bottom of the stairs and straight through the wall of the back kitchen. I can't believe it! There must be a rational explanation."

We never found one.

*The Duck with a Dirty Laugh told rude jokes to his friends*

# Chapter Four – September 1996

August 1996 was a record-breaker for the Loader family. First Chris and Linda were married at Longforgan in Scotland on August 2 and on August 29, Alex and Michelle tied the knot at Weaverham in Cheshire. As parents we enjoyed an unforgettable, emotion-packed month, watching with pride and lumps in our throats as our sons married young women who already felt like our daughters.

St Paradis played its part in the drama as well. Chris and Linda had arranged to spend their honeymoon travelling around the parts of Europe where she had lived as a youngster. They had scheduled a short stay at St Paradis, for old times' sake, since they had helped us to choose the property two years before. After an idyllic wedding, traditional Scottish reception and fairytale first few days of their honeymoon, Chris suddenly became ill with a virulent stomach bug, which made him far too wretched to want to stay in hotels. Rather than cancel the rest of the honeymoon, Linda drove from the Jura to the Limousin in one fraught day and they spent much longer than planned at St Paradis — where he could be ill in peace. They joked about not having intended to test the "in sickness and in health" part of their wedding vows quite so soon — but said St Paradis had been their salvation.

Alex and Michelle flew off to Barbados, where all went well. After we had collected them from the airport and taken them home to Weaverham we were able to think about our own plans for a holiday. We needed one! We had given our spare keys to our oldest friends Roger and Eileen (Roger and Jack had been at school together from the age of 11), and they were going to have a few days at St Paradis before we arrived. Roger had just taken early retirement and for the first time in their lives, their time was their own.

Once again we loaded the trailer in advance, leaving out the big settee and replacing it with two small Parker Knoll chairs which I had bought as auction bargains for £2.50 each. We put in the kitchen base units which we had regretted not bringing in May. Following our unsuccessful attempts to dry the washing the previous time, Jack had succumbed to my campaign to buy a tumble drier, so this was packed, together with our old television which we intended to use to show wedding videos to any French neighbours foolish enough to express an interest.

We took the pups to the kind friends who usually cared for them while we were away and then set off at 4pm on Thursday, September 19. The traffic was terrible, even on the parts of the journey which we could normally rely upon to be trouble-free and we did not reach Portsmouth until well after 9.30pm. For some Sod's Law reason the diesel foamed so much while Jack was trying to fill up the tank on the Peugeot that it took him ten minutes at the pumps. Quite flustered we checked in at the ferry terminal. The ship departed half an hour late in high winds and a big swell. Our cabin was out of order when we found it and we had to change it for another one. All in all, we were glad when we were eventually able to collapse on to our bunks and go to sleep, rocked by the waves.

Next morning we watched with interest while a Formula 1 motor-racing team disembarked. Our journey to the Limousin was slow because the trailer was heavy and we did not want to punish its small wheels too much. We stopped en route to look at the prices of worktops for the base units and were horrified to discover that what cost about £30 in England was anything from £50 to £120 in France. We decided to make our own tops and tile them!

When we arrived Roger and Eileen were well ensconced but freezing. They love France as much as we do and visit it as frequently but they prefer Provence — which is considerably warmer than the Limousin. Their Provençal accommodation has also never been a farmhouse with metre-thick granite walls and dark rooms. We felt rather guilty, especially as Eileen, a consummate cook and housewife, had applied "a woman's touch" to the house so that it was beautifully clean and tidy. Much tidier than it ever was when we were in residence. They had also made a delicious supper, just ready to pop into the oven.

Chris and Linda had bought us a blue oil lamp made at a local pottery and left us a sweet letter. We were pleased that the house had metaphorically stepped in to rescue their honeymoon from disaster.

Roger and Eileen said they hadn't seen Paul and Elisabeth and they were worried. Jack saw Michel going past to his vegetable plot and asked what was happening. Michel told him that Paul was in hospital for another eye operation and that his heart was not too good. Elisabeth was not at home. We were sad. Paul was very precious to us and to all his friends, and we didn't like to think of old age finally catching up with such an active and independent man. He always seemed so indestructible. It was only a few months since he had planted flowers in front of the house and barn – and lugged great blocks of stone around to make us a rockery. We hoped that this exertion had not contributed to the heart problem.

The following morning, Saturday, our Dutch friends Jan and Beatrice dropped by. They had just returned from a holiday in St Tropez, and we arranged that they should come for a meal on Tuesday. We saw Elisabeth's daughter, who told us that Paul's heart condition was not serious and that her mother was now at home. We went round and were pleased to see her in good spirits. She said the doctors were building up Paul's strength for the forthcoming operation and he was the life and soul of the hospital, having typically made friends with everyone! We asked her over for the evening to see the wedding videos. As we were about to go off to Stoc to buy some provisions, the telephone rang. It was Jack's cousin John and his wife May, who were holidaying in France. They asked if they could come to see us on Wednesday; and could we book them into a hotel as Roger and Eileen were using the spare room?

We decided that Fate had decreed this would be a social sort of holiday rather than a DIY session.

Sunday morning saw Roger and Eileen looking for a local church where they could go to Mass. The local priest travelled to different ones on a rota system but St Paradis, in its dusty splendour, never got a look-in.

When they returned, we decided to put the kitchen base units together. They were to go each side of the back kitchen. An easy job, we thought, especially as we had labelled everything before we took the dismantled components out of our friends' garage. Both Jack and Roger shared a professional love of practical things and could probably have assembled a nuclear power station over a couple of weekends, but the base units defeated them. Eileen and I offered advice which was rarely taken. By late afternoon, with everyone at their wits' end and patience wearing very thin, it suddenly dawned on us all that we had made a wrong basic assumption. The units could not have been laid out in a long line in the original owner's kitchen. They must have been in an L-shape...

By then it was too late to do anything holidayish so Roger and Eileen went outside to plant a fig tree they had bought us as a present, while Jack and I finished the now obvious assembly of the units by adapting the bits, which had gone round the L-shape, to go in a straight line.

We had beef stew for supper and afterwards spread the house's "treasures" out all over the dining table. These were things that Marguerite had "helped" me to find in obscure corners of the attic, in cupboards and stuffed in the fireplaces. We had never taken them back to England because they were so delicate that we were afraid they would disintegrate in a centrally-heated house. They included letters from the 1880s and 1890s, written in the days when you couldn't pick up the phone to pass on simple messages within a farming family, like "Can I borrow the threshing machine?" and "I'm ill, please help me get in the harvest", but had to rely on the postman. There were letters sent by Marguerite and her mother to her father when he was away in the Army during the First World War — and his replies written on the backs of the same paper. One told a story in patois — the ancient *langue d'oc*. There were textbooks which had belonged to Marguerite's uncle as a boy in the 1870s, religious books belonging to female members of the family where the s's were printed like f's, farming almanacs and a book in which the young Marguerite had practised elementary still life drawings using a soft pencil.

We spent the evening examining the documents and going over them with a dictionary, pooling our knowledge of French to try and make sense of the more obscure phrases.

Sorry that our guests had endured such a boring time the day before, I spent the next morning walking round the village with Roger and Eileen. It was dry and some of the paths which were normally impassable because of mud were explorable today. Jack prepared for the big engineering job of the holiday — making a hole in the massive back kitchen wall to accommodate the drains which he intended to install. Neighbours had suggested taking a pneumatic drill to it but we regarded that as a bit drastic. We didn't want the house to fall down.

At lunchtime M Lebrun came to see us armed with the architect's plans for altering the site of the burned house. We spread them out on the table and we all agreed that the walled garden which was planned would be a vast improvement on what was there.

After our meal, Eileen and I pottered while Jack and Roger attacked the wall. During the morning Jack had removed all the small stones in a hole with a volume of about two cubic feet. Filling the centre of the space was one big stone which just needed to have its mortar removed and then be manoeuvred out of the way. Jack could not believe his luck. He had had no leeway about where to make his hole, yet once again the house was "helping". He had allocated a couple of days to the job but with Roger's assistance it would probably be done in a couple of hours.

We celebrated by sitting outside round our picnic table and opening a bottle of wine, listening idly to the rural sounds of St Paradis. Birds, cows, dogs, tractors...

"There he is!" Roger exclaimed, suddenly.

"Oh, yes!" replied Eileen.

"Who?" we asked, mystified.

"The Duck with a Dirty Laugh," said Roger.

We were perplexed.

"We've heard him every day," Roger explained. "Listen. He's sitting on Mme Echelle's pond telling rude jokes to his friends and splitting his sides when he gets to the punchline. Then his mates join in."

And he was.

"Quack, quack, quack, quack, quack. WARK! WARK! WARK!"

chortled the duck, in the best bar-room fashion. We could picture his shoulders shaking with mirth and the tears of laughter being wiped from his eyes with a wing.

"WARK! WARK! WARK!" went the other ducks, as they got the joke.

After that we always listened out for The Duck with a Dirty Laugh. He had a good repertoire of stories and kept his friends thoroughly entertained.

The next day Roger and Eileen suggested that they would move on to the South of France before Jack's cousin and his wife arrived so that they needn't stay in a hotel. We had discovered that both hotels in the nearest town were closed for their annual holidays and there was nowhere else suitable for our guests to go. Roger and Eileen wanted to buy their own property in Provence and it had dawned on them that they could easily get out of season accommodation in their favourite village near the coast while they did some research on prices and analysed what was available. We envied them the freedom offered by early retirement and wondered how long it would be before we were in the same position of being able to go somewhere on impulse.

With typical generosity, they volunteered to cook the meal for Jan and Beatrice that night and produced a gourmet three-course dinner on our rather primitive equipment. New readers should know that the kitchen at St Paradis then housed a £200 Eastern European bottled gas cooker with a fierce oven and a useless grill, a fridge-freezer, a 20-year-old microwave, a meat safe, a long pine dining table with eight chairs, a leather sofa, a leather-topped writing desk, an armchair and a small pine table. Saucepans and kitchen utensils hung from a *batterie de cuisine* and the working surface beside the cooker was an old metal stand with a melamine top which had once held our goldfish tank. It was not exactly sophisticated.

During the leisurely meal, Jan and Beatrice told us that the six villages in our commune held a fête every July, and a big knees-up which was the equivalent of the English "beating the bounds" on May 1. They loved going because it made them feel that they really belonged to the community. We were sorry to have missed both events over the years and made a mental note that we should vary the dates of our holidays to fit in the various local festivities. We were ashamed that we hadn't even heard of one of the villages which was only three or four miles away but on a road we had never used.

Roger and Eileen left next morning, Wednesday. It was their 26th anniversary and a fitting day to start a search for their own French dream. Not quite so romantically, we decided to investigate our septic tank.

The only real plastic drain that the house possessed ran from the downstairs loo out through the back wall and under the garden to the septic tank. The porcelain sink by the front door drained via a black rubber hose through the front wall and on to the sloping path which ran along the front of the house. Water ejected this way ended up in Paul's flower bed if we were lucky. If the volume was too great we had to create a dam to divert it away from the Lebruns' drive.

We knew there was a septic tank because we had a thin pipe from the back of the loo which ran up the rear wall and vented noxious smells at roof-level. (We had French friends whose pipes vented noxious smells at nose level, but that was another matter).

We had never been able to find the tank but it had been located for us this time by a combination of Paul who had caught the plastic drain with a spade while gardening, and Roger, who had then followed the drain as far as the concrete block which rested on top of the tank.

Jack dug down to the tank itself and I video-ed him, prepared to make a mucky film that The Duck with the Dirty Laugh would appreciate. We didn't know what to expect and were relieved to discover a modern plastic construction with three chambers protected by a red plastic cover. When we removed the lid it didn't smell at all and the bugs inside, which we encouraged from time to time with a special chemical that we put down the loo, seemed to be doing a grand job. We made precise measurements of its distance from the old stable and the hole in the back wall so that we could find it again in years to come when the garden had been constructed above it.

We went over to see Elisabeth and she said that Paul was having his operation. She was waiting for news. We crossed our fingers and popped back regularly to check up. The operation took five hours, to everyone's consternation, but Paul was reportedly OK afterwards. No wonder they had needed to build up his strength. As always, we were impressed by the French health service.

John and May arrived in the late afternoon and we showed them round proudly. We had already bored them to tears in England with photos of the house and stories of how we had renovated it. Once again, the "treasures" came out for examination after supper.

They insisted on taking us out for a meal the following night and asked us to book somewhere. They were going to spend the day with a friend who lived near Limoges.

Next day while John and May were away we went up into the attic and attached pins beside two big cracks in the walls on either side of the house. They had been there for a long time but we were unsure if they were getting bigger. Rather than rely on eyeing it up, we decided to be scientific and do some measurements.

Then we tackled a job which Jack had been relishing. We cleared out the cellar.

In his dreams it had been an easy task if messy — but gloriously messy in the way little boys (aged 52) love. In theory it involved turning on the pressure washer and washing all the rotten wood shelving, which had made a rich compost on the floor, out of the drain hole in the left-hand corner, in one wonderful whoosh...

In practice we found that the drain-hole was not only below ground but also too small to take the particles of wood. We had to dig out the compost, which was several inches deep. The whooshing would have been done standing up, from the cellar steps, but the digging had to be done doubled up, under the arched roof. It was not such fun after all.

Jack dug the stuff out with a big snow shovel and handed it up to me through the cellar window. I stood outside in the garden and disposed of the contents of the shovel, inserting it back through the window when it was empty. Some of the bits of shelving were quite big and I put them on the bonfire.

A long time later, Jack had his moment of glory with the pressure washer and we were gratified to see the stone floor of the ancient *cave* being revealed. Part of the room was lined with stone but the rest had been hewn out of the living granite on which the house was built. We left the cellar trapdoor open to allow the circulation of as much air as possible, and then wedged the front door to the salon open too.

During our exertions we had taken a few moments off to telephone a posh local restaurant and book dinner for four. We were amused to think that it would be our first meal "out" since we had bought the house. We had been so busy over the past two years that it had never occurred to us that we might do anything so profligate. After all, the money spent on a meal might buy several drainpipes or some reels of cable...

We had an excellent dinner and had to ask the waitress to explain some of the more obscure items on the menu. We were glad we checked about the *cervelle de veau* before we accidentally chose it. I knew that *cerveau* meant brain but I didn't realise that *cervelle* meant brains!

It was early and only two other tables were occupied. It was nice to be eating in a restaurant frequented by local people which wasn't at all touristy. We thought the staff might be quite surprised to be serving English people like us, who had adopted *La France Profonde* so readily.

A young couple was shown to a table behind ours and suddenly the unmistakable sounds of Middle England emerged. We listened dumbfounded. In a totally out-of-the-way place in the back of beyond, the English diners now outnumbered the French.

As we paid the bill our fellow countrymen attracted our attention and we went over. They said they were staying with the husband's mother in her nearly-restored farmhouse in a speck on the map whose name we didn't recognise. We knew there were quite a few Dutch home owners around the area, but we had never heard of another English person. That we should all choose to go to the same restaurant on an out-of-season Thursday night was quite extraordinary.

Back home we showed John and May the wedding videos. John had been to Alex's wedding but May had been at the opera in Italy at the time. They got their own back by showing us film of their grandson's christening. A lovely nostalgic time was had by all.

After our guests had driven away we discovered May's handbag in the kitchen. Jack jumped into our car and by dint of knowing the back roads was able to "head them off at the canyon" — in other words block their way at a road junction a mile or two away and hand it over.

We went to the capital of the *département* to visit the bank, the supermarket and the *bricolage*, to return some plastic drainpipe bends which Jack had bought by mistake. He's an excellent plumber but his mind goes a blank in French DIY shops and however long he gazes at the plumbing displays with a mesmerised expression on his face, you can practically guarantee that he will buy the exact opposite of what he really needs. French pipe sizes and fittings are all different from English ones and knowing how he would do a job in England is a positive disadvantage when it comes to tackling one in our adopted country. Diagrams on the back of an envelope don't help. Shop assistants in our favourite stores hide when they see us coming if they know we are on a plumbing binge. Home again, Jack rolled up his sleeves and started to dig the trenches for the various drains. I got out a new tin of brown gloss and painted the door to the bottom of the stairs and the wooden wall between the kitchen and the back door. I was delighted with the result as the fresh paint in the original colour made the kitchen timeless rather than dowdy and dated.

The following morning we went over to Elisabeth's to see how Paul was getting on and to find out when he would be coming home. To our amazement he was sitting in his accustomed chair at the kitchen table, having returned from hospital the previous evening. He was in good spirits but there was blood on his cheek where an instrument had been used during the operation and his eye was half-closed. We were full of admiration at his resilience and courage. We were pleased to accept an invitation for supper that night from Elisabeth.

Then we sped off to the nearest city to purchase some more plumbing bits and to exchange the ones we'd bought by mistake. We also bought four square metres of light brown tiles to cover the working surfaces in the back kitchen, and a Le Creuset-style cooking pot, both for a fraction of what we would have paid in England.

That evening we had a tasty and convivial supper with Paul and Elisabeth and were delighted to meet his youngest daughter, who dropped in with her husband to check on Paul's wellbeing. During the meal he showed us a book that had been produced some years before by a local writer. Each page featured a photograph and a write-up about a wellknown character in the *département*. Naturally no book of this sort would have been complete without a piece on Paul: it seemed to us that he was known and loved by practically everyone between Limoges and Clermont-Ferrand! The article was affectionate and the photo showed him in characteristic pose behind the bar at his old bistro, a welcoming grin on his face and his cap firmly on his head. We were thrilled that he had gone down in Limousin history in this way.

Another photograph stuck in our memories. It depicted an old shepherdess wearing wellingtons, standing in a field, accompanied by a sheepdog and surrounded by sheep. She was knitting. This bucolic and timeless scene was made rather incongruous because she had obviously decided to look smart for the photographer and was wearing her best coat...

*Some of the hamlet's tiny narrow lanes seemed so private that
I felt more like a trespasser than a villager*

# Chapter Five – September 1996

Next day saw us still beavering away. With me as labourer, Jack had already run the plastic drainpipes from the back kitchen and bathroom along and down the interior walls so that they popped neatly out of the hole in the thick back wall. This had involved using rapid-setting PVC glue which gave us about a couple of seconds' leeway to get the angles on the joints exactly right. It was quite a fraught operation. Then he had replaced the stones in the hole and remortared it so it was as good as new.

Now he was digging trenches to take these drainpipes. The foul drains were destined to link into the septic tank while those for dirty water only were due to end up — one day in the future — connected to a long length of yellow plastic land drain which we had bought through a newspaper small ad in Cheshire and brought over in the trailer. It was supposed to run in a trench to a soakaway in the field.

Unfortunately Jack had found out the hard way that while the job he had expected to take days — making a hole in the house's thick granite wall — had only taken a few hours, the one he had dismissed as the work of a few hours — digging about 20ft of trenches — was going to take several days. He had badly under-estimated the problems which would be caused by the stony ground. Every spadeful of earth contained several stones or small rocks which had been covered by a thin layer of topsoil. These were a nuisance and were separated out and thrown on to a grow-ing pile destined to make hardcore for the terrace foundations. The big problems were caused by large boulders under the sur-face which lay directly in the line of the trench. If he couldn't manhandle them out of the way using leverage, he had to break them up with a sledge hammer and cold chisel. If they still failed to yield, he had to attack them with an electric drill until they cracked along a fault. One monster was so large and stubborn that he gave up hope of removing it and spent an hour or two cutting a drainpipe-sized gap in it. It was very slow and frustrating work, as well as a hard, physical slog.

When I was not required to help him, I continued to paint the doors and door-frames in the kitchen. The inside of the front door was particularly pleasing to do, as it was very old and intricately-made. Places where the wood had shrunk to reveal daylight had to be filled in. Every surface that was changed from dull pre-war brown to the same colour in a shiny clean version added to the transformation of the kitchen. The effect wasn't modern and it certainly wouldn't have adorned any pages in a lifestyle colour supplement, whose experts would have decked the room out in a fancy pastiche of a "period" style quite foreign to its past. No interior designer would have looked at the kitchen and recommended that we should choose such a genuinely old-fashioned, unfashionable colour: but it felt right. It was as though the house was preening itself and returning to its heyday, when it had been a bustling family home and its occupants had picked their colour-scheme from the limited range available to them.

While I was painting Jack called me outside to look at a very strange phenomenon. It was a glorious day with a cloudless blue sky and bright sunshine. He pointed upwards, and standing out in silvery contrast to the dark green of the tree foliage in the back-ground, we could see hundreds of strands of what appeared to be long cobwebs, flying in the air at roof-height and up into the sky. They shimmered and twinkled as the breeze caught them, wafting them to and fro. We managed to capture them on video but we had no idea what had caused them, unless they were made from spiders' silk.

Also enjoying the wonderful weather were the lizards who lived in the crevices of the stone blocks which made up the walls of the house. I loved watching them. One of my secret desires when buying a house in France had been to have one sufficiently far south to harbour its own lizards. They lived at the front and the back, as their forebears must have done for a couple of hundred years. The front ones resided where the mortar had crumbled in the join between the house and the bread oven building and also in cracks beneath a stone bench which ran below the kitchen window and had been used by generations of inhabitants as a place to sun themselves and gossip. The ones at the back had their homes in the nooks and crannies of the henhouse and stable, which we rarely used. When the sun came out they would run up the walls and bask in the warmth, their legs spread-eagled and their little feet clinging on effortlessly. When we made a movement they would skitter shyly behind the leaves of the vine or fig tree until they decided it was safe to emerge. They were so well camouflaged that when they were motionless we had to look hard to pick them out — usually they caught our eye only when they made a dive for an insect or decided to change position. We loved them, like the *cicadas* and sunflowers, because they were so un-English: they were a constant reminder that we were in France and just that little bit nearer to the Mediterranean.

We didn't love the other inhabitants of the ancient vine which climbed over the front of the house. It produced small dessert grapes, tart and packed with seeds, which we harvested every year but rarely consumed. It played host to hornets — *frelons* — buzzing gladiators at least an inch long whose sting could be pretty serious. They hovered lazily around the bunches of ripe grapes and often blundered into the kitchen through the open window where they flew threateningly round the room until Jack could zap them down with specially-strong insecticide. I was too frightened to spray them: I thought they might get their retaliation in first. They were very aggressive and fought each other to the death in the air and on the ground where they rolled, viciously jabbing and stinging. We sometimes wondered if the fermented juice from rotting grapes made them drunk. I wasn't particularly bothered about our snakes — we had grass-snakes and had once seen a viper — but I was afraid of the *frelons.*

After lunch Jack was bored with "mining" his trenches and decided to do some work in the bathroom. The windows were in a poor state. When we had bought the house the guttering above the bathroom window had been broken for years and water had poured down the wall every time it rained. The back of the house faced north and bore the brunt of most gales and heavy rain which swept across the open fields. The "waterfall" from the guttering had washed away the mortar and made the wall damp, permeated behind the shutters to rot the window frames, caused the catch to seize up and worn a triangular hole in the stone window ledge. Mending the guttering had been one of the first jobs we tackled, so the situation had not deteriorated over the previous two years.

Now Jack removed the pair of narrow windows by lifting them off their hinges, took out the panes of glass and dismantled the woodwork, cutting out the rotten parts. I went down into the stable at the back and carried up a "spare" window that we had found years before in the salon. It too was probably 100 years old: the same design and roughly the same size. We used parts of it to patch up the original windows, which Jack glued and clamped.

Late in the afternoon I made a hot-pot in the new Le Creuset-type container and cooked it slowly in the oven. The result tasted wonderful and I was an instant convert to that method of cooking. My indispensable French pressure cooker was now joined by another vital utensil to be used practically every day in France and England — a heavy enamelled cast-iron casserole.

Next morning, Monday, while I was putting the finishing touches to the painting in the kitchen, we had a flying visit from Jan and Beatrice. They invited us round to their home for a coffee later in the week and passed on the sad news that Paul had had a bad night with his eye. We saw the doctor arrive later and were very sorry that our brave old friend was suffering. We slipped over for a little chat but mostly kept out of the way because we didn't want to be a nuisance.

The repaired windows had glued nicely and Jack replaced the panes of glass. He ran out of conventional putty half-way through the job and finished it with some synthetic stuff in a tube which we had bought as an experiment. It was messy and when it had almost dried I had the job of neatening everything up. Most of the panes were original and it was interesting to see how wavy they were in comparison with modern glass made by the float method. If I looked simultaneously through an old pane and a new pane, then moved my head up and down, I could see the image of the landscape rippling and distorted in one and perfectly consistent in the other.

Jack lit a bonfire to burn the all weeds he had dug up whilst making his trenches. It smoked lazily most of the afternoon then bucked up and burned with proper flames during the evening when everything had dried out.

While we were in the kitchen doing the washing up after lunch, there was a scratch at the door. When we opened it, we found Gitane on the doormat, squirming as always with antici-pated pleasure. She came in and we made a fuss of her. Suddenly she squeaked in pain and we saw that she had blood on her back from a small wound. Then there was another scratch and we found a black and white pup at the door. He had a docked tail and the head and figure of a fox terrier, though his coat was wrong for the breed. We had seen him running round the village with Gitane and her daughter but he hadn't introduced himself. We invited him in too and he immediately pee-ed against the table leg. We shooed him out crossly. None of our doggy friends had done that deliberately before, though Gitane sometimes widdled herself out of pure excitement. It struck us that we hadn't seen Betty lately. She lived with her shy elderly missus in the next occupied house on our side of the street and was usually a daily visitor and scrounger of titbits.

We heard Mme Echelle calling from outside her house a couple of hundred yards away. Her voice carried in the still air and Gitane responded at once. We opened the front door and she ran off to her mistress. The pup, who was waiting outside, wandered away in the opposite direction, ignoring the shouts which became louder and more annoyed as Mme Echelle advanced down the street, a switch from the hedge in her hand, swishing ominously. We couldn't understand what she was calling. It sounded like "Mee-lo" but we later found out it was the pup's name, "Milord." She waved the switch at him and he came to heel, crestfallen.

We went out for a chat in the middle of the road, St Paradis-fashion. She said Milord was always in trouble and that she had to teach him some manners before the other villagers gave him a swift kick up the backside. She'd rescued him from some sad fate we didn't catch and he had joined the canine family down at the old *auberge*. She said Gitane's wound was the result of a tick and that Betty wasn't around because her owner was ill in hospital. Suddenly it seemed that life was not being kind to two of the vil-lage's stalwarts. Our neighbour had lived in St Paradis all her life and had been a good friend to Marguerite. It seemed inconceiv-able that she wasn't in her little cottage, pottering about in her blue pinny.

We spent the most of the afternoon and evening crawling around on the bathroom floor. Before we could do anything creative or ambitious in there we had to make the floor level. The original floor was constructed from hand-cut oak planks which had warped over the years and it was very uneven. We had been given some heavy-duty plastic foam designed to go under parquet flooring and we stapled this down over the planks. Then we manhandled large sheets of industrial quality chipboard into place on top and covered the floor entirely, screwing them down at regular intervals, hoping that we were going into the massive beams below and not just through the floorboards. We had a time-and-motion system for doing this — Jack drilled the holes for the screws, I went round afterwards with a lighter drill to countersink the holes and then he put in the screws with a screwdriver attachment on his big drill. Cutting the last sheet so that it fitted exactly was a work of art, given that none of the walls in the room were straight or true. Jack wasn't satisfied after we had screwed it down and he decided to take it up and pare a little off one edge, which was a pain at the time but sensible with hindsight. The house had always "helped" with the other rooms and projects, but we had been so slow with the bathroom that we sometimes got the impression that the house regarded it is an unnecessary frippery which didn't deserve any luck.

Next morning I did the washing with our geriatric washer and spin drier. Then after lunch we went to the capital of the *département* to visit the bank, *bricolages* and hypermarket. We were looking for a new telephone. We had asked for the cheapest handset when we had the line installed but the one France Telecom had given us was quite sophisticated and expensive to lease. We could buy one for the cost of about nine months' hire. We compared all the models available at the various outlets and plumped for a special offer on one with an answering machine which only cost a few francs more than the ordinary telephones. We thought it might come in handy if we were waiting for a message from home but couldn't avoid going out somewhere. In spending mood, Jack treated himself to a small gas welding set with some money he'd been given for his birthday three and a half months previously!

Back home we unplugged the original telephone and installed the new one. As if on cue, Alex rang and we were able to prove that it worked. The answering machine had to be plugged into the mains and there wasn't a handy socket. We also chickened out of recording a message — should it be in French, English or both — and decided to let that go for the time being.

On Wednesday we decided to go to the city to buy a double-basin ceramic sink to go in the back kitchen. We had investigated prices at all the DIY stores we frequented and had found the one which represented the best value for money. It wasn't a very exciting purchase for Jack, he was more interested in tools and building materials, but for me it represented a milestone in the rehabilitation of the house. I had never been a fan of housework, although I enjoyed cooking — especially in France with the ingredients that could be found there — but I found it hard going to do the food preparation, washing up and general cleaning with no proper working surfaces and only an awkwardly-positioned porcelain sink with a cold tap. A back kitchen with modern facilities, connected one fabulous day in the future to a hot water system, was my personal goal.

As usual we faffed about and didn't get to the city until about 11.25am. Then Jack procrastinated over the copper plumbing fittings he needed and it was 11.50am before we grabbed an assistant and asked if we could have the ceramic sink of my dreams. No, he said. We couldn't. It was so close to lunchtime that the warehouse out the back would be ready to close by the time he could walk over there and it would certainly be lunchtime by the time he had found the right sink. We must come back when they re-opened at 2pm.

There was nothing we could do but we were incensed. We were going to spend about £80 and we objected bitterly to killing time for two hours while the staff enjoyed their lunches. We were however faced with the full weight of French culture and protest was useless.

Seething, we went out to the car park and got into the car. The city was grid-locked as thousands of employees dashed home for a meal. We thought we would drive out to a nearby spa town visited by Roger and Eileen, which we had never seen. It took us 20 minutes in traffic jams before we reached the city outskirts from the commercial centre where the *bricolage* was sited. As always we ranted about the stupidity of a country which more or less closed down for two hours when its businesses could have been making lots of money — like the few enlightened hypermarkets which found it well worth their while to stay open.

We were in no mood to enjoy the spa town. Roger and Eileen had laughed about the fact that they had driven out there specially, inspected the hotels, discovered that they could have a bathe in the warm spa waters and had bemoaned the fact that they had nothing suitable to wear. Back at St Paradis they had realised that their swimming things had been in the boot of the car all the time, in a bag which they had forgotten to unpack.

Just after 1pm we found ourselves in the city again, having driven to the spa, around it and back in a boring hour. Then we remembered that Mammouth, one of the hypermarkets, would be open. We could wander round there for a bit.

Fate had obviously decided that this should happen, for when we got to the store we discovered that it had just taken delivery of a consignment of young fruit trees from Holland which were a bargain price and appeared to be in excellent condition. We had intended to buy some during this holiday to plant in a row in the back garden, to define the border between the garden and the field and to act as a wind-break when we were sitting outside. We had almost given up hope of finding any, as Roger and Eileen had been told when they bought the fig tree from a garden centre that other fruit trees would not be available until around mid-October.

We bought two apples, a pear and a cherry. They were about 5ft high and we had fun wheeling them in a supermarket trolley to the checkout without sweeping away all the hanging overhead signs and posters.

By the time we'd searched for other bargains it was the magic hour of 2pm and we returned to the *bricolage* for the sink. The one I had decided to buy was slightly the wrong colour but met all our other criteria. The assistant went to the warehouse for one like the example on display and came back most apologetic. They had none left that colour, he said. Would this do instead? He pulled open the box and there was a sink in exactly the shade I'd wanted. We began to think that perhaps things were going right after all.

In St Paradis we learned that Paul had gone back to the clinic that day for a check-up and in spite of the problems he'd experienced earlier in the week, the specialist was pleased with his progress.

We staggered into the house with the heavy sink and put the unwieldy box down on the salon floor. Then after an oddly-timed meal, we devoted the rest of the day and evening to our favourite objects: drainpipes.

The following morning I helped Jack to fill in the trenches and rake the soil over them so that the garden was as good as new. Milord came to watch. We let him stay with us outside but forbade him to go into the house in case he did any more widdles. He was an intelligent little dog with an air of street-wise quick-wittedness. This time when the call for "Mee-lo" echoed round the village, he scampered off in reply.

Jack asked me to dig the holes for planting the fruit trees and while hole-digging is not my forte I didn't have the heart to protest. He'd had more than enough digging to do over the past week or so.

The first hole, nearest a large sycamore, was almost impossible to excavate because the ground was so hard. I could hardly get the spade in, let alone manipulate it. Each of the other three holes became slightly easier to dig as the ground became more moist. We were afraid that the sycamore would take too much water out of the soil, but we were committed to our line of fruit trees and we thought we would see what happened. Other trees even nearer the big one seemed to have survived quite well. We planted the young trees in the holes and watered them in profusely. Then we resurrected some old barbed wire which had originally surrounded the farm garden and used it to fence off the fruit trees, to protect them from the worst that any visiting cattle or horses could do to them.

It was a sunny day so I went for a saunter round the village with my camera. I was building up a collection of photographs which showed St Paradis in all its moods and every sort of weather. Each time we came there were subtle changes. Some of its tiny narrow lanes seemed so private that I felt more like a trespasser than a villager.

That evening we went round to Beatrice and Jan and admired the new road which had been built up to their entrance by the commune. They were pleased to have a better surface but sad to lose the profusion of wild flowers which had lined the old track and the grass which had grown up along its centre.

Friday was our last full day in St Paradis and we spent it socialising! The Vallets came at 11am; Paul, Elisabeth and Anne-Marie at 6pm and then we went back to the Vallets at 7.30pm. The hours passed in an alcoholic haze of conviviality. We showed Paul the video we had taken of our progress on the house and garden, which he had not been well enough to witness in person, and he rewarded us with "Oh la la's" of appreciation.

In conversation he mentioned that the two women who had bought the house behind Elizabeth's had heard that the vendor of our house might have a wood to sell in the village. They had asked if we could give them his address, because they wanted to buy it.

We didn't know the name and address offhand but we had it on the title deeds to the house. We had never met the vendor, Marguerite's second cousin, who had inherited the house by a roundabout route, because we had used a proxy to sign the *acte de vente* on our behalf. We promised to look up the information.

Later that evening, when we were alone, Jack said: "If there's a wood going, I want us to buy it. I've always wanted a wood. Let's write to the chap ourselves."

In the middle of the night I woke up thinking I heard footsteps on the stairs. Marguerite had been completely absent during the holiday but suddenly the thought flashed across my mind: "I hand you over to the living." The familiar tingle up my spine returned.

# Chapter Six – New Year 1997

We arrived home happy and relaxed. We'd had a productive time at St Paradis, our sons were happily married and now owed their first allegiance to their new wives. After 25 years of being primarily responsible for them, we could take a back seat and concentrate on ourselves.

I had been made redundant as a local newspaper editor exactly a year previously and my little business of short-run book publishing and freelance writing was going well. I wasn't drawing much income from it but the venture was self-sufficient and each project financed the next. People were getting to hear about me and there was no shortage of customers. I joined with a friend who had a printing business and we bought half-shares in a digital printing machine to produce my books. My future looked rosy and interesting. Jack was over the magic age of 50 and working his socks off, as always. If his employers offered him early retirement and a golden handshake he would be pleased to accept it: we could spend more time at St Paradis then.

I went to stay with Chris and Linda and wallpapered their bedroom in the bungalow they had bought a few weeks before their wedding. They were trying to transform the interior from the 1970s to the 1990s but long hours at work meant it was a slow job for them. It reminded me of how my parents had come to help us when we had our first house in Southampton as newly-weds. I felt as if I had moved into a new era of my life: grown-up, my own boss, experienced and fancy-free.

As we'd promised ourselves, we wrote to the previous owner of the house at St Paradis, Jean-Luc Martin, asking if he really did have a wood to sell and if he would name his price. We said how much we adored the house and outlined some of the work we had done on it.

He wrote back saying that he did not want to sell any of the land which had belonged to Marguerite's family farm. He wanted to keep his inheritance together, and had only sold us the meadow because it joined the house. However he was really pleased to hear about what we had done. The letter was so friendly

**65**

*We were getting through two barrowloads of logs a day*

that I replied almost immediately with lots of photographs: of us, of the boys' weddings and of the basic restoration we had done to the house and grounds. I told them how interested we were in Marguerite and Alain, and described a little of our telepathic experiences with Marguerite.

Thus began a correspondence and a rewarding friendship which has grown ever since. It's private but it's very moving. Jean-Luc and his wife Geneviève have welcomed us with affection and trust and say we are like long-lost members of their family. They tell us that it is quite extraordinary and uncanny: we have done everything at St Paradis that Marguerite ever wanted. They have even given us, and our heirs and successors, the free use of a nearby wood. We can see it from the back of the house. Truly, Marguerite "handed us over to the living."

We had six weeks of carefree innocence between Alex's wedding on August 31 and The Bombshell.

We had noted that my dear 88-year-old mother had been getting increasingly forgetful and seemed to say some rather strange things. She was very deaf but had always been extremely active: we'd had to stop her using her bicycle a few years before because she kept hurting her legs on the pedals when she pushed it along. She lived with her sister-in-law, my aunt, in Lincolnshire. Jack and I travelled over to spend the weekend with them three or four times a year. We tried to chat on the telephone at least once a week and when we hung up the receiver we would remark to each other on how well — or badly — Mother had responded to the conversation. If we'd had a pretty incomprehensible time we would blame it on the deafness or slight memory loss.

At the end of October the real situation became apparent. Things were much worse than we had ever suspected.

Mother had developed a fixation that "men" were living in the roof of the house and were plotting to take the house and her money away from her. Her bedroom was on the ground floor and she was sure she could hear the men outside, saying bad things about her and the family. She wanted to report them to the police; to get her solicitor to stop them saying these things. She became too frightened to sleep downstairs. Then she began to hear "sirens" and "warnings" in the middle of the night. She had been in charge of the ARP ambulance service in the town during the war and these memories started to resurface, distorted by a brain which was no longer functioning properly. She couldn't understand why people down the road didn't evacuate their houses when the "siren" sounded and messages came over the "public address system" which she could hear so clearly inside her head. Nothing could persuade her that these delusions were not real. She spent every waking moment worried and hunted, often trying furtively to pass on vital messages — in notes or whispers — without the men finding out.

It was devastating.

I drove the 130 miles over to Lincolnshire most weekends. The person who now inhabited my mother's body was not the one I had known and loved so dearly for 48 years. The new personality was a cruelly twisted caricature which magnified my mother's few weaknesses and obliterated her wonderful qualities. To see her like this was worse than seeing her in physical pain.

Her general practitioner started to treat her and called in a consultant psychiatrist who specialised in senile dementia. My aunt bore the brunt of everything bravely but the strain was terrible for her and we knew it was just a matter of time before big decisions had to be made.

I couldn't sleep when I was with Mother because she would roam around the house with a torch looking for her persecutors, or come and tell me all her imaginings. I knew my aunt humoured her but I couldn't curb my journalist's instinct to argue rationally about the sirens and announcements. Of course, she didn't believe me and simply argued back. I couldn't sleep when I was at home in Cheshire because I could imagine what was happening in Lincolnshire and I knew how shattered my aunt was becoming.

It was with all this hanging over us that Jack and I decided to go ahead with our planned annual New Year at St Paradis. We needed to recharge our batteries before we could face what 1997 was going to throw at us. We knew in our bones that it was going to be bloody awful and we yearned for a peaceful start to the year. We always had such a great time with Paul and Elisabeth and we hated to be parted from St Paradis for very long. If we didn't go now it was unclear when we could go again. People said we should be selfish and think of ourselves: so with Auntie's consent, we did.

The weather was bad all over Europe as we set off on Friday, December 27. The trailer as always was heavily laden with tools and stuff for the house, all roped down under a tarpaulin. We had bought some snow chains for the car, just in case.

We were almost the last to disembark from the ferry at Le Havre the following morning. It was freezing and the fields alongside the *péage* were covered with snow. We were glad of the hot coffee served with our breakfast of bread and croissants at the usual stop in Normandy.

Jack turned on the radio. It was the second Test Match in Zimbabwe. He was thrilled but I was not. I am not interested in cricket. I can see the skill and bravery in it but I don't understand the rules. It's so *slow*! Tennis on the radio I love. I can visualise it happening. Cricket on the radio I regard as a waste of airtime. Something happens once a minute if you are lucky. It lasts ten seconds. The remaining 50 seconds are filled with verbal wallpaper from commentators who feel they have to fill the silences. By Sod's Law, every time we go to France and can only receive long wave on Radio Four, there is a Test Match. Honestly. The cricketing authorities time the things deliberately. I swear they ring Jack up in advance and arrange the Test Matches to coincide with the Loaders' visits to St Paradis. We listen to cricket en route and whenever we are in earshot of a radio when we get there. I tolerate it because I love him...

Between Evreux and the Limousin, for hours on end in a surreal snowy landscape, we heard the usual garbage from the hearty commentators and 20:20 hindsight from a certain Yorkshire bore as they watched the teams battling it out in sunny Africa.

In the little town which boasts our Stoc supermarket we have a choice of route. One way goes via the normal main road and the other follows our Favourite Drive in the World. For sentimental reasons, and because the trailer would be pointing the right way for easy unloading at the house, we chose the latter. As we drove through one hamlet in the commune, a mile or two from home, we saw a large newly-butchered pig suspended from a front-loader of a tractor. The carcase had been split open and two farmers were dealing with it skilfully on a triangle of grass in the centre of the village. The scene was a strange mixture of ancient and modern and we were talking about it when we rounded a bend going uphill almost in sight of St Paradis. It was too late to stop before we hit the sheet of ice which completely covered the road. A stream had become blocked, burst its banks and spilled all over the lane before freezing in the sub-zero temperatures.

We were stuck. Even if Jack could have got some purchase for the estate car, the trailer would have held us back. He managed to uncouple it, but it was so heavy — and the ground was so slippery — that for my part I didn't have the strength to guide it in the right direction at all. It jack-knifed across the ice. The car threatened to slide back. It was almost impossible to stand up without holding on to something. We were now a real traffic hazard, although few vehicles used the lane and there was no telling when the next one might come along. It could have been in two minutes or five hours. If it was coming downhill it would be quite unable to stop and we would have an interesting pile-up on our hands.

It was late afternoon and getting dark. The snow wasn't more than an inch deep. While Jack stayed with the car to warn oncoming motorists I volunteered to take a short cut over the fields at the back of our house and then search for help in the village. As I trudged over our two-acre field in my thick shoes, I spotted horse droppings and piles of hay. As usual, the meadow had been occupied by an unknown "guest" until the very last moment before we arrived. It was the biggest field in St Paradis and our agricultural contractor friend Georges, who looked after the land for us, liked to make the best use of it.

I went round to Paul and Elisabeth. They would know what to do. They were entertaining a friend called Jean and an elderly deaf man. As true Good Samaritans, Paul and Jean came to our rescue immediately, not even stopping to put on their coats. Paul was still in his carpet-slippers and we were very worried about him catching a chill or falling over on the lethal surface. It was far too cold to be out with only a woolly for protection against the bitter temperature, especially for an octogenarian. Jean used his car to tow our Peugeot uphill off the ice, and succeeded after a lot of revving and slithering. Then we manhandled the trailer so that it was off the ice downhill and pointing away from St Paradis. Jack drove a mile or so "round the block" to pick up the trailer and we hitched it on. Paul and Jean went back to the welcoming warmth of Elisabeth's house and we said we would join them when we'd retraced our steps.

We stopped first at the house to pick up a bottle of whisky from the larder as a present for Paul's kind friend. We would have been in dire trouble without him. Sadly he had gone by the time we went round and Paul refused to accept the whisky on his behalf. Jean had been happy to help, he said. I stopped for a quick Ricard and a chat while Jack went back home to start unpacking the trailer. Paul apologised: the water in our house was frozen and he hadn't been able to prevent it. Everyone in St Paradis was suffering the same problem.

I returned to help Jack. Paul had, as always, lit a log fire for us in the kitchen. It looked cheery but didn't seem to be having much effect. We looked at our electronic thermometer. It registered -7.6°C outside and 2.6°C in the kitchen. It was probably colder in the rest of the house.

I went upstairs to turn on the electric blanket to air the bed.

Jack investigated the stopcock in the barn. We always turned the water off there between visits and drained down the system in the house. Paul was right. Everything was frozen in spite of the pipes being insulated with thick plastic foam and covered with a blanket of straw. Jack unpacked his blow torch, removed the black foam and started to thaw out the copper pipes. He got them to the point where water would come out of the tap in the barn, but it would not flow through into the house.

The phone rang. It was Elisabeth, inviting us round for a supper of hot soup. We were very grateful and thanked her profusely. She laughed.

"We're friends!" she said. "I know you'd do the same for us."

Revelling in the warmth of the homemade soup and the heat in the small kitchen, we chatted and swapped news. Paul had undergone another operation on his eye, which seemed to have been successful. We never ceased to be impressed by the efficiency of the French health service, in comparison with the poor old creaking NHS.

We were sad to hear that Betty's owner had died. What would happen to the village when everyone of her generation had passed away?

Elisabeth said the cold had been very bad and her house was freezing outside the warm kitchen. Her daughter-in-law had bought her a long flannelette nightie for Christmas!

When we finally returned home the bedlinen which had been in a plastic sack in the trailer was so cold that we had to warm it up in the tumble drier before we could put it on the bed. We used two duvets: one of 15 togs on top for bulk and insulation and a 4.5 tog one underneath to mould to our bodies. We left the electric blanket on.

We woke the next morning at 9am, having slept surprisingly well. When Jack went downstairs the water had frozen again. We decided not to attempt to wash for the time being and had coffee made from milk and bottled Evian water. The kitchen was 1.6°C and outside it was –7.7°C. We relit the log fire in the big *cantou* fireplace and put on two portable gas heaters at full blast. By 10.20am the room had reached 9°C. I was like a Michelin woman in salopettes, thermal underwear, numerous jerseys and a body-warmer. Jack had on his long-sleeved thermal vest, lumberjack shirt, Irish fisherman's sweater, body warmer and woolly hat.

We created a festive atmosphere in the kitchen by putting Christmas cards from our French friends on the high mantelpiece over the fireplace and fixed a holly wreath to the salon door to show our neighbours we were in residence.

In England I had enlarged Marguerite's head and shoulders from her wedding photograph and framed the resulting picture. We hung on it on the kitchen wall opposite the front door where she seemed to gaze on all our activity with wry amusement.

Jack got the blow torch and went to thaw out the pipe in the barn again. There was a blockage somewhere which was preventing water coming into our one tap over the kitchen sink, so we gave up on that and turned the stopcock off to cut the connection.

The tap in the barn, once used for the animals, was our only source of water.

We filled saucepans and buckets with water and carried them through into the kitchen so that we could cook and carry out domestic chores like washing-up. We put a bucket of water in the loo so we could flush it manually, so to speak. We heated any hot water we required on the gas cooker, as always.

Outside we saw that the bad weather had forced M Lebrun's builders to give up work. Their lorries had made a mess of our grassed frontage and there were piles of sand, stones and rubble everywhere covered with a dusting of snow. They had removed all the remaining walls of the burned house, which had originally abutted the gable end of the Lebruns' house. They were in the middle of building breeze blocks up against this wall to square it off, and presumably as a base to give it a nice rendered finish eventually. The scaffolding was still in place. The masons had also started to build a new stone wall to go round the site, using the stones from the old walls. We knew from the plans that it was due to have ornamental railings on top. We had asked if the men could save any stone they didn't need, because we wanted it to build a terrace at the back of the house, but instead they had put the unused pieces down as hardcore on the muddy little road which ran between our property and the Lebruns'.

The vine which covered the front of our house and part of the barn had spectacular icicles hanging from it and the water in the stone drinking trough boasted a thick layer of ice on the surface. The water we had eventually used to wash up the breakfast things had solidified into a glacier on the path by the front door.

Elisabeth telephoned. Paul was out and she couldn't get rid of her bathwater — perhaps Jack could use his blow torch to heat up the waste pipe? We went over together and discovered that the pipe in question was plastic, which rather put paid to that idea!

Jack went into their cellar and found that none of the pipes there was insulated. He daren't leave them like that, as the weather was worsening, and wrapped our own fibreglass insulation round them, in spite of Elisabeth's protestations that it was too much trouble. It was a long job and she gave us lunch of *charcuterie* and steak with boiled potatoes as a gesture of thanks.

The temperatures continued to drop. It registered –9°C outside and when we returned to our kitchen the gas fires were hardly coping. The thermometer hovered between 5-6°C. We lost all our energy and Jack had diarrhoea. He said he felt very strange.

Betty came to see us. Her late mistress's daughter and family were staying in the neighbouring house. We hoped it was warmer than ours.

Hardly feeling inclined to do anything, I started a letter to the Martins, using a rudimentary French translation programme on the old computer by the fireplace in the kitchen. Jean-Luc and Geneviève were in a centrally-heated apartment in Paris and I thought they might be interested in our rural plight. I wondered how Marguerite would have coped. At least when the house was occupied all the time, the granite walls would not have acted like a fridge — as they were at present.

Jack went into the salon and put up his woodworking equipment. His first priority was to build an insulating "cupboard" of chipboard around the pipes in the barn so that it could be packed with rockwool. He spent many hours on the task, getting chilled to the bone in the barn where there was no heating at all. I wanted to keep him company but he said there was no sense in us both being frozen.

After a pretty miserable day we couldn't get to sleep when we went to bed at 10.30pm. We had left the electric blanket on its lowest setting all day, just to keep the bed aired. I lay in the dark under the mountainous duvets and tried to talk to Marguerite in my head. Would she show herself to me, like she had fleetingly to Jack? I gazed into the blackness. Nothing happened. Then the thought shot across my brain: "It's not going to be *that* easy!" I was ashamed.

Next morning I woke up and as I surfaced from sleep I heard three people breathing in different rhythms... One of them obviously wasn't me. One might have been Jack. Who were the other two? I never knew if it was significant or not — but it was spooky. Our bedroom had been the one occupied by her parents.

It was bitterly cold and Jack was still feeling unwell. The kitchen had dropped to 1.6°C overnight and the water to the tap in the barn was frozen again. We had run out of food so we drove to Stoc via the main road to buy groceries and a regulator to allow us to use a third portable gas fire which we had bought second-hand in England. We met Elisabeth's daughter Anne-Marie and a Dutch woman friend who, like us, had come to St Paradis expecting the usual convivial New Year. We felt odd and lethargic. Our minds were just ticking over. I forgot to get my mushrooms weighed and priced in advance, causing an embarrassing delay at the checkout and a clucking of French housewives behind me in the queue. I usually loved shopping, especially for French food. Now eating was no longer a pleasure — just something you did to stay alive.

It started to snow gently and the landscape became white as we drove home. The snow settled on the back lanes but turned to slush on the main roads. I decided everywhere looked so beautiful that I would put on my wellingtons and take some photographs. Standing by the front door I was struck by how pretty the green and red wheelbarrow full of firewood looked against the grey salon door, with its green and red holly wreath. I took several shots of this and the front of the house then picked my way down the side past the pigsties and out on to the meadow. I found that Georges had cut two new drainage channels to tackle the endemic sogginess of the field caused by the old blocked-up pond. The channels were about nine inches wide and threaded across the field, covered with ice and snow. From the bottom of the meadow I photographed the back of the house against flurries of snowflakes. I thought of trekking back to the site of our drama with the sheet of ice but decided against it as the snow became heavier.

As I walked home I decided that the exercise in the fresh air had done me good. I was raring to go. I prepared a beef casserole for our evening meal and served up a quick lunch of soup, bread and cheese. Jack cleaned up the gas fire, put on the regulator and turned it on. We had another ally against the cold in the kitchen.

Jack started to box in the water pipes along the salon wall where they fed in from the barn to the kitchen. He found that the cold was affecting his metabolism and he was working much more slowly than usual.

75

We turned on the French radio news and a reporter said that the present cold spell was the worst in Europe for a century. We telephoned Alex and asked him to turn off the water supply to our garage in Cheshire in case it froze. At St Paradis our bottles of olive oil had gone solid and we put them on the ledge of the bread oven, to the side of the fireplace, to thaw them out. We kept our boots and slippers on the edge of the hearth, to keep warm. The ballpoint pen I was using to record my daily diary would hardly write and we were burning a lot more wood than usual. Luckily Paul had arranged a delivery of logs for us during the autumn, for we had nearly finished the original four cubic metres (known as a *corde*) which we'd bought two years before.

Like everyone else in the village, we stayed indoors while the snow settled outside.

The following day was New Year's Eve.

Fascinated, I watched a fly which had survived against all the odds. Crawling over the sink it drank the dregs of whisky left in my glass and the drops of red wine in Jack's. It deserved them. Washing up last night's dishes did not have priority when water was so hard to come by.

Overnight the outside temperature had dropped to -12°C. We went over to Paul and Elisabeth to find out if they needed any shopping. We were going to see the New Year in with them that night. When we returned with their list and went into the barn to get the Peugeot we found that it wouldn't start. It was too cold. We remembered how exactly two years before, Paul's son-in-law had driven us miles to look for second-hand furniture and electrical goods. That wouldn't have been so simple today.

Not sure if the problem was frozen diesel or a flat battery, we tried to warm the engine with a hair drier and cursed that we had left our battery charger in England. Michel came past, saw our predicament and lent us his heavy-duty charger. He told us his wife wasn't very well.

Gitane came to pay a call and was glad to snuggle down by one of the three gas fires. We got the impression that her kitchen was probably even colder than ours.

I took the charger back to Michel when the car had come back to life and was shocked to see how ill his wife was. I hardly recognised her. She said she was waiting for the doctor to come.

We drove to the capital of the *département* and managed to visit the bank, two supermarkets and a DIY store to get all the things we needed. Our purchases included a heavy-duty battery charger, to be left permanently at St Paradis! Once again, the country lanes were covered with snow but the main roads were OK.

When we returned I heated some precious water from one of the buckets and washed my hair in the porcelain sink by the front door. Then I made a *crème brulée* with *crème fraiche,* mango, strawberries, cherries and brown sugar. The sugar had hardened into a block and I had to put it in the liquidiser to separate it back into crystals. The *brulée* and some specialist English cheeses were our contribution to the evening's meal.

We went to Paul and Elisabeth's at 7.45pm. Our fellow guests, their old friends Cécile and Robert, and their Dachshund, had not arrived. We counted the charming couple as friends, having met them several times at St Paradis social events. They lived in Paris, had a family house in the local spa town and had known Paul since his days in the bistro. The dog was another story. We loved dogs and they usually loved us, but this pooch was different. It was easily frightened and had bitten Jack's leg and hand the previous New Year, so we were not keen to encourage a repeat performance. We kept well out of the way.

Cécile and Robert arrived late. Instead of our usual New Year glad rags, we were all muffled to the necks in our thickest informal clothes. Cécile, normally an elegant exponent of the revealing little black dress, was in a thick black trouser suit with added thermal layers. They echoed our story. Their old house, like ours, had soaked up the cold while it was unoccupied and was now inhospitably chilly. Their water supply was frozen. So far they had not enjoyed their winter break in *la France Profonde* and they were threatening to cut it short and return to the Metropolis.

The meal, as always, was great. I always felt inadequate when faced with expert Continental cooks. Robert prepared their contribution of oysters, while Elisabeth put the finishing touches to her dishes of *langoustines* followed by *pintade* with chestnuts and *petits pois* and rounded off with fruit salad. My *brulée* went down well but the unusual English cheeses were received politely but without much enthusiasm. I should have stuck to the classics like Cheshire and Stilton rather than try things with oranges and herbs in them. We drowned our sorrows with Muscadet, Côtes du Rhône and champagne and had a thoroughly convivial time, except for when the Dachshund went out for a wee and came back with frozen paws. Distraught, Cécile wrapped it up in her expensive coat and put it on a chair from where it surveyed us dolefully as we ate, whimpering occasionally.

During the meal, which made us all feel more positive and sociable, we arranged with Robert and Cécile that we would drive over to their house in the spa town, with Paul and Elisabeth, in three days' time — to have lunch and compare houses.

Just before midnight, Elisabeth's Dutch family and several friends came round to see in the New Year in the traditional manner. Things were slightly less ecstatic than usual. Anne-Marie's friend, whom we had met in the supermarket, had tipped her car into a ditch. Anne-Marie, the passenger, had hurt her head and leg. Like us, they had hit some black ice on a corner. It looked as if the car might be a write-off. If it was, getting back to Holland would be pretty complicated.

As her friend was telling me this, she absentmindedly put her hand out to stroke the Dachshund's head. It got her in the twinkling of an eye. She pulled her hand back and blood started to drip from her bitten fingers. We went home to get some sticking plasters.

If these were the omens, it certainly didn't seem as if 1997 was going to be much good for anyone.

# Chapter Seven - New Year 1997

On New Year's Day we stayed in bed until nearly 10am. We'd got to bed about 1am. There didn't seem much point in getting up out of the warm. It was 1.6°C in the kitchen (at least it was consistent) and –8.9°C outside.

We rang Mother and Auntie to wish them a Happy New Year. Mother was totally confused and Auntie was at the end of her tether. She needed me in Lincolnshire the moment we got home. I started to worry again.

I went across to Paul and Elisabeth to thank them for their hospitality, pay for the firewood he'd bought for us and check that everything was all right after the previous night. We sat chatting round the kitchen table, getting through Paul's supply of red wine while Elisabeth sympathised with me about my worries. They confirmed that Anne-Marie's friend's car was *une perte totale*. The only good thing about the bad weather was that it did make everyone solicitous of their neighbours and ready to help with any problems. We were all in it together.

Jack spent eight hours out in the barn, getting colder and colder, and slower and slower. He had decided to move the water pipes so that they ran at a different angle which would not be so prone to icing up and to remove some which were now unnecessary.

To insulate his face and because he felt so lethargic, he had stopped shaving and it was interesting to see his beard creeping up his cheeks over the places he usually shaved. I thought it made him look like Captain Birdseye and actively encouraged him: he was all furry and cuddly like a Polar explorer. The effect was enhanced by the fact that like me, he kept his woolly hat on indoors to stop any unnecessary heat loss. I was still rotund in my increasingly grubby *salopettes*. We made a glamorous couple!

In the middle of the night I was taken ill with diarrhoea and sickness and Jack went down with identical symptoms a few hours later. Elisabeth rang up to say she was ill: she was suffering from the same bug, too. We agreed to call off the visit to Robert

*The commune's snowplough had pushed up high banks of snow*

and Cécile the next day. Later she rang me back to say that they were so fed up with the conditions in their house that they had decided to return to Paris immediately.

Chris telephoned from Majorca where he and Linda were spending the New Year in a rented villa with her parents. The weather there was positively tropical in comparison to ours and they were having a marvellous time. We were glad someone was.

I stayed in bed most of the day and Jack joined me when he was able to be out of sprinting distance of the loo. We lay miserably side by side. To add to our discomfiture, we had to use the bucket of water to flush the lavatory. Every time we thought the holiday couldn't get more disastrous, it did.

I was so cold I didn't know what to do with myself. I had my side of the electric blanket on the highest setting, wore a dressing gown over my nightie, hiking socks on my feet and clutched a hot water bottle. I wished I'd got some wincyette pyjamas too. I passed the time by reading a paperback copy of Mrs Gaskell's "Cranford" which is supposed to have been set in Knutsford, near our home in Cheshire. I couldn't get comfortable and had constant backache.

That night I was almost delirious. Sleep wouldn't come — just wild, meaningless thoughts going round and round my head. It was horrible.

Next morning, Friday, January 3, we forced ourselves to get up. We were due to leave the following day and there were things which had to be done however lousy we felt. There had been a heavy fall of snow overnight. We had to clear a path from the salon door to the barn so that we could reach the logs for the fire. We were burning two wheelbarrows' full each day.

We wondered if our stomach problems had been caused by the fact that the fridge had stopped working and we'd got food poisoning. I discovered some meat which had gone a disgusting shade of green and when we tested the temperature inside the fridge it was much higher than it should have been. In fact, it was warmer than it was outside. We remembered that we hadn't heard the motor running for days. Food wasn't even cold to the touch. Jack deduced that the part of the kitchen where the fridge stood was so cold that the thermostat no longer responded properly. He over-rode it and the motor started again. We chucked out the most suspect food.

The snow was beautiful and somehow not like English snow. Weak as we were, we could shovel it up quite easily — it was light and powdery, and no weight at all. It cloaked everything in soft contours. The ugly heaps of builders' rubble now resembled gentle hillocks and our meadow was a carpet of dazzling white interrupted where the short black stumps of fence posts protruded through. Only the top few inches were visible — the rest was under drifts of snow.

Paul came across with a parcel of presents from Georges and a copy of the commune newsletter. A new woman mayor had been elected and she was doing a great job modernising the running of the little community. We found her newsletters fascinating and looked forward to them. Georges was a councillor and presumably he was expected to distribute the newsletters to households on his patch. We supposed he hadn't brought the things in person because he'd heard on the grapevine that we were ill in bed.

Suddenly I heard an unaccustomed noise: water dripping from the tap in the kitchen! The ice which had blocked the pipes had finally melted, thanks to Jack's unceasing work on insulating and warming the water system. He had boxed it in all the way from the barn so that the pipe was now in a seven-inch square insulated duct with a gap along its centre through which he could blow hot air from the hair drier. He rushed to turn on the stop cock and we had a ceremonial flush of the loo before I took a photograph of him triumphantly turning on the tap over the sink. We felt as though a weight had been lifted from our shoulders.

We needed to buy some more bottled gas, as we were using it at a tremendous rate to heat the kitchen. We had kept the car battery on charge and were reasonably sure that it would start. As we were preparing to get the car out of the barn, we saw the villager who had "helped" Jack to make our well cover 18 months before. We now knew, sadly, that he was an alcoholic — getting through about four bottles of wine a day. He had a shopping bag with him and he was only wearing light clothes. His trainers had holes in them and were soaking from walking in the snow from his home not far away.

He asked if we were going to the town and if we would give him a lift. How could we refuse? We were sure he was going to buy some drink and that his family would not be pleased. On the other hand we couldn't let him walk two miles in each direction in old trainers with holes, when the snow would have been up to his ankles. We had no doubt that the urge for drink was so powerful that he would have crawled to the nearest booze shop, regardless of the conditions.

Jack drove very carefully into the town. It was hard to tell where the road stopped and the ditches began, but we made it. We arranged to meet the villager outside the Casino supermarket when he'd done his shopping and we'd completed the transaction on our gas bottle. When we went to the agreed meeting place, he wasn't there. I searched the town centre on foot and met Elisabeth's son, Vincent, who asked if we could give him and his little boy a lift through France back towards Holland the next day. I replied that I was afraid we wouldn't have enough space and explained that we were looking for our passenger. Just as we were about to give up, he turned up, having bumped into Vincent who'd told him where we were. My annoyance evaporated when he gave me a bunch of roses to say "thank you" for the lift. It was so sad. He was basically a very nice man, in his late thirties or early forties, who was destroying himself with alcohol. He'd had numerous "cures" which hadn't worked and everyone predicted that he would drink himself to death. Yet he had spent money, which would have bought him a bottle of the wine he craved, on some flowers for me!

As we returned home, it started to rain. We were apprehensive. The last thing we wanted was for the snow to melt and then freeze again.

We went round to Paul and Elisabeth so Jack could finish insulating the pipes in her cellar. Vincent popped in with his son, to leave their cat in his mother's care while they returned to Holland. I said we'd had second thoughts: if they didn't mind being squashed up, we might just be able to get them in the back of the car. We could take them as far as Orléans. He thanked us but said he really needed to go straight to Paris where he could catch a train to Amsterdam. He would go all the way on the train, as he had originally planned.

None of us relished the journeys we were due to make the following day.

Mme Echelle came round to wish us a Happy New Year. She apologised for not visiting before and said she had been ill — as had nearly everyone else at her end of the village. They either had the 'flu or sickness and diarrhoea. Perhaps the fridge wasn't to blame for our problems. Was it just a "bug" or could the village water be contaminated?

That evening we watched the thermometer in consternation as the outside temperature fluctuated around 0°C. Would that mean more lovely sheet ice in prospect for the morning? We packed the trailer and kept our fingers tightly crossed.

Next day, Saturday, we did the last-minute filling of suitcases and were nearly ready to go at 10am when Paul and his friend Charles came over. Charles was from Paris but he was retired and spent a lot of time with his mother-in-law and grandchild in St Paradis. The two men told us it was impossible for us to leave because the whole of France was paralysed and the autoroutes were impassable. Charles had abandoned his own plans for driving home.

We couldn't believe it. We had been to the town the previous day without too much trouble. We had to go, we insisted, our ferry ticket was booked.

Gently but firmly, they told us to listen to the French radio.

We turned on France-Info, which does a rolling news service every 15 minutes. The country was at a standstill. There was snow in the centre, black ice in the north and avalanches in the east. The south had seen its first snow for years and only the south west was not *paralysé*. Special mention was made of the autoroute we needed to take between Vierzon and Orléans. It was so dangerous that it was closed to all traffic. Even if we could get out of the Limousin we couldn't get any further.

I was ready to cry with frustration. Our ferry was booked on a debenture-holder's deal which could not be changed. Mother was worse and Auntie needed me. Why was fate throwing all these problems at us?

Jack looked at the tickets to see if there was a telephone number to ring. Surely no one could reach the ferries today? The management might show some compassion to stranded travellers.

He couldn't believe his eyes. The ticket bore the next day's date. Someone along the line had made a mistake which we hadn't spotted, but at least it was in our favour. We could stay in St Paradis for another day with a clear conscience.

The rush of adrenalin which had carried him through the prospect of driving across France evaporated and Jack began to feel ill again. We stayed indoors and pottered about, not moving far from the fire. I had stripped the bed in readiness for leaving and we decided to change our mattress for the new one on the spare bed. I still had constant backache in bed and wondered if our mattress — which was 25 years old — had just given up the ghost.

In the early evening Paul invited us over to watch the news and weather forecast on their television. The reports showed numerous cars overturned in ditches and long traffic jams stuck single-file on the snowy motorways. Prospects for the next day seemed no better.

Elisabeth said that when Anne-Marie and her partner Martin had taken Vincent to catch the train in the city at 7.30am there had been a complete white-out. The 20-mile journey in Martin's builder's lorry had been a total nightmare.

Back home we had no energy to do anything worthy. We sat and listened to nostalgic LPs from our youth while Jack dismantled the old television we had brought from England to show the wedding videos. He decided that the tube had gone and it was beyond repair.

Jack was really ill in the night with bouts of violent diarrhoea, which left him weak and shaky. We both knew he was in no state to drive anywhere. We couldn't possibly leave with him in this condition. There had been heavy snowfall during the night which once again looked tantalisingly beautiful. The snow was now about knee-deep and it was impossible to tell exactly where the road was on the bend outside the house. I stood on what I thought was solid ground and dropped straight into the ditch.

We had France-Info on constantly. The country was in chaos. The autoroutes were still closed and emergency centres were being set up all over to deal with travellers who had become stranded. Servicemen were told they need not try to return from leave and children were warned not to start school the following day. The whole of Europe was gripped in appalling freezing conditions. We felt that our own personal drama was a little piece in history's giant jigsaw.

We heard a car nearby rev up and creep out of the village. It belonged to Betty's family. Later we saw it being towed back by a tractor. It had only reached the first corner, by Michel's farm, before sliding into the ditch. We knew then that we had no option but to remain where we were. The decision had been made for us. The lanes were obviously impassable.

We went outside to examine the latest snow. It was well above the tops of our wellingtons, which made walking around in it a rather damp experience. It was the deepest I'd ever known.

Jack was slowly clearing a path from the salon door to the barn when Paul rapped on the window in the house opposite to catch our attention. We strode over, leaving enormous bootholes in the snow. Thoughtful and hospitable as ever, he was determined to give us half their joint of veal and some cheese to keep us going. He knew we had eaten nearly all our food. We had only bought enough to last until the previous day and we'd thrown quite a lot of that out.

Charles joined us for a drink (there is always a drink on offer there!). He had come to carry in the couple's firewood. Jack dug a path from the road up Elisabeth's drive, and another from the back door to the wood store. I marvelled that however ill he was, he always pushed himself to keep going.

Not long afterwards, public-spirited Georges battled past on his way round the commune, a snowplough lashed to the front of his tractor. He cleared the road, pushing high banks of snow up on either side. The route was very narrow but better than nothing.

Back with Paul and Elisabeth we said we might have put the snow chains on the car and chanced it, if we could have been sure that no one would have come in the other direction. But Anne-

Marie and Martin, who phoned Elisabeth while we were there, said they had spent the day pulling vehicles out of ditches with their lorry. They didn't recommend taking the risk. Jan and Beatrice telephoned her too, from Holland, saying that the famous Dutch skating race on the canals was being held for only the 15th time this century. We watched it later on the television news.

We telephoned Alex and asked him to look in our filing cabinet in Hartford and find out the terms of our ticket purchase and an emergency number to ring. We also asked him to get in touch with Auntie to say we were stuck and would get home as soon as humanly possible.

Then we took the snow chains out of their plastic case and tried to work out how to fit them. They were tangled into a cat's cradle and had to be separated. We had expected to find four, but there were two — for the driving wheels only. We couldn't remember off-hand if the Peugeot was front or rear wheel drive and had to look it up in the manual. Then we spent a good hour experimenting to find the best way to fix the chains on the front wheels. They were supposed to be "quick-fit" but you could have fooled us.

When Alex gave us the ferry number in France we tried repeatedly to get through. Eventually we reached someone who said they couldn't suspend the ticket so that we could simply turn up at Le Havre when the weather improved, but they could transfer it to another specific date. Later in the day, after hearing a favourable forecast on the radio, we arranged for it to be made valid for the following night's sailing. We asked for a cabin and the chap said he would confirm this when he could get through to the reservations computer. They were faced with mayhem at the booking office. Presumably their staffing levels were suffering as well, with people stranded all over the country who should have returned to work from their Christmas holidays.

Now that our arrangements were settled, we felt happier. Jack wanted to do some gentle DIY, so we made a working surface for the left-hand unit in the back kitchen by glueing together four layers of chipboard. We intended to tile it another time.

I cooked a pot roast supper with Elisabeth's veal joint. Her meat was always better quality than ours because she bought it from the butcher in the next town. I was too scared to do that because I didn't know what cuts to ask for. Suddenly we realised that we were enjoying our food for the first time in days. We agreed that whatever had been wrong with us had finally gone. We went to bed at 10.30pm and slept soundly.

The following morning the rolling news programmes confirmed that French life was returning slowly to normal, though the weather forecast was bad for later in the week. We had a "window" of a day or two which we must use. The autoroutes were open, although drivers were urged to take the utmost care. We decided we couldn't risk towing the trailer because it would be too much of a liability. We unpacked it, stuffed the estate car with everything we needed, and left the rest behind — including Jack's bulkiest tools. Sadly, he would have to live without the wood-working equipment for a few months.

We put the chains on the car and went to say goodbye to Paul and Elisabeth. Paul said there was a 30mph speed limit on cars fitted with chains, which we thought would slow us down enormously. We envisaged having to keep them on for a good part of the journey.

We left at 10.45am, inserting ourselves into the narrow groove cut in the snow by the commune's rudimentary snowplough and praying that no one would come the other way. The chains made the car feel strange and the steering wandered around rather worryingly, but progress would have been impossible without them. Creeping by Michel's we could spot where the other car had gone into the ditch.

The road out of St Paradis was still virgin snow and we guessed we were the first to tackle it. When we reached the T-junction with another road leading into the town we could see that the few passing vehicles had compacted the snow so that it was very icy. We crawled along cautiously, the chains providing a little traction on the slippery surface. A false move and we would have been in the ditch too. By this time we were resigned to what Fate might throw at us and instead of being scared we marvelled at the sheer beauty of our surroundings. The large lake on the right, covered in matt grey ice and bordered by leafless trees clothed in brilliant white snow, was quite breathtaking. A big bird of prey launched itself out of the branches and swooped low over the lane.

As we neared the junction with the main road to the town we negotiated a bend and met a car coming in the opposite direction, far too fast. It was outside the cemetery, which was handy, as there was a narrow parking area in front of it where the ditch had been culverted. We were able to swing to the right knowing that it was still solid ground, and the chains enabled us to keep going in the deeper snow. The other car was being driven by a young man. He swerved, hit the bank of snow, reversed out and carried on. We were astounded that anyone could be so stupid.

At the junction we discovered that the main road was slushy but quite passable. We had known it much worse on previous holidays. We no longer needed the chains but there was nowhere we could pull off to remove them. The road had been cleared by big snow-ploughs which had banked up the snow on either side, so there was no access to lay-bys or frontages. It was not possible to drive more than 30mph with the chains − even if we had wanted to − because of the effect they had on the car and we presented a hazard to impatient French motorists who wanted to overtake us. Eventually we pulled on to the car park at Stoc and I went to buy some biscuits while Jack took off the chains.

We carried on to the city almost normally, agreeably surprised that the dangerous part of our trip had been so short. We had needed the chains for only two or three miles, but without them we would still have been stranded at St Paradis. We felt relieved and keen to get on, now that the worst was behind us.

In the city we pulled into a familiar left-turn, governed by traffic lights. We had to drive over some snow. When the lights changed, Jack accelerated on to the inner ring road and I heard a strange noise. It reminded me of something that I couldn't place. Then I remembered. It was the sickening thud of a flat tyre.

I wound down the window to have a look. The passenger side rear tyre was punctured. It was such an arbitrary, cruel blow on top of what we had already endured that I wanted to take Fate by the throat and ask why the hell it was fooling with us like this. I wanted to laugh hysterically or burst into tears. I didn't, of course. We pulled as far as we could off the road and onto the snowy forecourt of a school for lorry drivers, which was closed for the holiday period. I helped Jack to take all the stuff out of the back of the car so that we could get at the hatch to the spare wheel. We piled the luggage on the roadside. Passing vehicles sprayed us with slush. Jack got filthy half-lying beside the car on a makeshift mat but he managed to change the wheel. As always, undoing the wheelnuts required almost superhuman strength and lots of leverage.

It was nearly 12 noon. The time when France closes for lunch. That was the most infuriating thing of all. We couldn't afford to waste two hours before the tyre was replaced, but we daren't carry on without an effective spare wheel. The tyre had been punctured by a large piece of jagged metal — obviously debris from an accident at the traffic lights which had been hidden by the snow. Similar booby-traps might lie all the way to Le Havre.

We decided to cut our losses and go for a McDonald's. It would fill part of the two-hour wait and we had to eat sometime. We didn't realise until we got to the restaurant just how disreputable we looked. The other diners were neat families on shopping trips or trendy students having a quick lunch. We were not only in our Scott of the Antarctic gear, ready to tackle any polar ice-caps between St Paradis and Le Havre, we were also filthy and monumentally fed up. People edged away from us as though we might contaminate them.

After we'd eaten we decided to look for a tyre depot. We remembered a *"Speedy Pneus"* en route to our favourite *bricolage* and thought we would wait on the forecourt and grab the first person back from lunch. When we arrived, it was open! We thought we were hallucinating. A French business, offering a vital service, open at 1pm? It seemed impossible.

We went to reception and approached the desk.

"We need a tyre..." Jack started to say.

"Sorry, sir, we haven't got any snow tyres left," interrupted the man, getting his retaliation in first.

We explained that we just wanted a new tyre. Any old tyre. The cheapest. The quickest. Now!

They were as speedy as their name. The tyre was fitted immediately.

We were back on the road at 1.45pm and turned on to the autoroute at 2pm.

We had an uneventful journey as far as Orléans. We stopped as usual for a rest and a trip to our favourite hypermarket where we bought a newspaper. The front page carried pictures of a car on its roof, a snowplough and a queue of stranded vehicles at a *péage* toll. Several pages were devoted to the local "weather story" inside. It was different from our experience in the Limousin.

We read that Orléans had been at the centre of the worst black ice, caused by *"chûtes de pluie verglaçant"* (freezing rainfall) covered by a dusting of snow — a lethal combination if ever there was one. There had also been fog, which must have been terrifying.

The headlines said that numerous cars had been wrecked in the rural areas, there had been many minor accidents and the emergency services had been stretched almost to breaking point. Side roads and pavements were like skating rinks. Trains were delayed and schools were closed. Sporting and social events were cancelled. Some postmen had managed to do their rounds, others found their vans wouldn't start. Those who should have delivered the mail on foot were told not to try. It was almost impossible to distribute daily newspapers. Lorries were unable to make deliveries of fresh produce and the city's buses had been forced to stop. The *département* could only afford to salt or grit the main routes, so national traffic was now on the move but local trips were very difficult.

At one of the two main hospitals — nominally only for children — a nurse was interviewed. She had worked non-stop for 20 hours in the accident and emergency department on Saturday (the day we intended to go home), when 146 people had been admitted. Most of them were elderly. They had ventured out to buy a *baguette* or some milk and had fallen heavily on the ice, breaking limbs or sometimes fracturing their skulls. The other hospital had treated 160 people on Saturday. Its director paid special tribute to the nurses, paramedics and radiographers who had coped with the emergency.

Two hundred drivers — a record number — had been stranded in wrecked cars in the countryside and had been rescued by the police or fire brigade. Even a police car, on its way to deal with an accident, had hit black ice and turned over several times.

Photographs inside the paper showed people attempting to walk on the city's pavements — and failing. They were pictured sliding on their knees or hanging on to street signs for support.

The most extraordinary story sounded like something from Gerard Hoffnung. At 7am on Saturday, a heavy lorry, trying to get into a petrol station on the RN60 road, had failed to stop and demolished the "super" and "unleaded" pumps. Half an hour later, a second lorry skidded and flattened the diesel pump. A hundred litres of fuel had escaped but fortunately there had been no fire or explosion. Two hundred yards up the RN60 the driver of another heavy vehicle carrying a load of pallets had lost control. The skidding lorry had uprooted about 50 feet of crash barrier before ending up on its side in the ditch. Interviewed, the proprietor of the petrol station said he was going home to have a good cry.

We left Orléans at 5pm and arrived at Le Havre at 8pm, in plenty of time for the ferry at 10.30pm.

We agreed that the holiday had been an experience. Character-building, maybe. We had survived unscathed, after all. But it hadn't been the nice restorative start to 1997 that we had longed for. If this was a foretaste of what was in store for the coming year, perhaps "hanging on and surviving" was going to be its theme.

# Chapter Eight – May 1997

The day after we returned from France I drove over to Lincolnshire for what were probably the worst ten days of my life — to date, anyway. My aunt was shattered. I was amazed that she had lasted so long. Our lifeline was that Mother had said she wanted to go into a home and had set her heart on one which was just around the corner. She was too frightened to stay in her own house any more.

She was very ill. She refused to go to bed at night and was just dozing upright in a chair in Auntie's sitting room. My aunt hadn't had any real sleep for nearly a fortnight and was absolutely exhausted. Because she never lay down in bed, Mother's legs were ballooning up with fluid collecting round her ankles. The "men" were an ever-present threat: they were plotting to steal her deed box and to sabotage my car. She was completely irrational, wandering round at night in a coat, scarf and boots so that she could oversee an evacuation of the street; mystified that no one else in the cul-de-sac was paying any heed to the dire announcements "the authorities" were making. I lay awake most of the night just waiting for her to come into my room with her torch, peer through the window in great distress and ask about the sirens.

It was so upsetting to see Mother like that that I felt physically ill. With hindsight I think I was going through a period of grieving which could not have been more intense if she had actually passed away. She had been the sweetest, kindest, sanest person all her life — what had she done to deserve this living hell?

The GP agreed to back us in our request to Social Services that Mother should go into an old people's home as soon as possible. I didn't know the procedure but I was so desperate that I unwittingly cut corners with the county council and DSS and got things done quickly. Her social worker was very helpful. By a miracle, there was a vacancy at the home Mother had picked and the proprietors agreed to take her in spite of the dementia. I fixed the moving-in date for two days hence, regardless of the consequences for the bureaucrats. I felt that if my aunt and I had to cope

93

*Architect Tony Garnier's futuristic designs were painted on to
the gable ends of the blocks of apartments*

for one more day we would both crack up.

Installing her was a major achievement. The idea was fine in theory but she couldn't cope with any sudden changes of routine. A mixture of bullying and cajoling finally combined to get her in there on the appointed date.

I went back to Cheshire. Auntie visited Mother twice a day at the home.

Things went well for the first fortnight. It seemed that the men hadn't followed my mother. But soon they caught up with her. They started to talk outside her bedroom window and then moved into the roof space of the bungalow building. Their accomplices "broadcast" defamatory radio programmes about Mother and her family through "loudspeakers" all over the home. She had a blazing row with one of the other residents and then became convinced that they had all ganged up against her and were trying to get rid of her. She refused to eat with them. She was certain that the men would kidnap her and dump her in France. Her handbag was packed ready to deal with such an eventuality.

The pain went on, and on and on. It was unbearable for everyone.

After six weeks, a kind neighbour, a consultant in charge of the psychiatric department at a nearby Cheshire hospital, suggested that Mother was suffering from paranoid schizophrenia, associated with her senile dementia. He was sure that she could be helped at the hospital's psycho-geriatric day unit. No one in Lincolnshire had ever put a name to the problem but the tentative diagnosis — later proved right — made everything fall into place. I read in a book that it particularly affects old ladies who have spent their lives putting other people first, empathising with others' problems and trying hard to please everyone. It was a thumb-nail description of my mother.

So we brought Mother over from Lincolnshire to live with us, and Auntie came too, for prolonged spells, to look after her. After initial assessment by a psycho-geriatric specialist, she started at the unit in April. Judicious use of the right drugs held the delusions and paranoia more or less at bay and Mother relaxed again. Her memory was very bad and she was not her old self, but she was no longer the driven and frightened new self. We took life a day at a time.

On May 8 we thought it was safe to leave her with Auntie and go to France for a rest. Our New Year visit had turned out to be energy-sapping rather than reviving: we were desperate for a break and some time on our own. The holiday was timed to combine a stay at St Paradis with a trip to our twin town of Mornant near Lyon to celebrate the tenth anniversary of the twinning. Jack and I were chairman and secretary respectively of the twinning committee and were responsible for organising our part of the visit. The French were due to come back to us in July for a twinning festival organised by Vale Royal Borough Council and the local twinning committees.

It was such a relief to be away that for the first time in three years at St Paradis I failed to keep a detailed daily diary. The twinning celebrations and forthcoming festival had involved us in so much letter-writing and planning over the previous months that I subconsciously rebelled against being orderly and well-organised. I just wanted to flop and never think about anything complicated again. I wrote up the notebook in general bursts of information, often many days apart. Jack was justifiably quite cross with me afterwards that we no longer had a meticulous record of what we'd done.

For the first time in years, we arrived at St Paradis *sans* the trailer. We had been forced to leave it behind in January, and with it much of Jack's woodworking equipment and various tools which he had — of course — needed urgently at home. The plus side was that we had a worry-free journey.

The highlight of the early part of the holiday was a visit from the Martins, who had a *maison secondaire* in a village about 30 miles away where they spent the summer holidays. Jean-Luc had inherited it from his parents. We had exchanged many letters since our first approach about buying the wood and we'd sent them photographs of our adventures over the New Year. Meeting in person sealed the friendship. They brought us a beautiful pink hydrangea which we planted in the front garden. We showed them the house proudly and then sat round the kitchen table talking about Marguerite's family and examining copies of various old documents which they had brought with them. They had a list of the land which they possessed in St Paradis: each plot or field had a number on the cadastral plan of the village. Some of the woods were rented out but others were unused. They said we could take firewood from any of these unspoken-for ones which we fancied, and manage the land on their behalf.

Jean-Luc and Geneviève had been very close to Marguerite. They told us how the house had been furnished when she was there and all about her personality. It was fascinating but we have respected their wishes to keep it private.

While we were having our tea there was a violent thunderstorm. It rained so hard that rain came through our bedroom window, poured through the gaps in the floorboards and ran down the kitchen wall! We had to dash upstairs and close the shutters to stop the cascade.

It was still cold at St Paradis. The weather was all to pot. There had been a long dry period and our poor little fruit trees, bought the previous September, had suffered from lack of water. Their leaves had also been burned by frost and they were in rather a sorry state. We hoped they would recover eventually. Paul had planted a row of sunflowers, some pumpkins and lots of marigolds for us.

The meadow had been retarded by the drought, too. The grass was just beginning to recover but it would be a considerable time before Georges could cut his crop of hay. The oak trees which had been eaten and rolled on by the visiting bull and his family nearly two years before were recovering but still tiny.

During this trip we wanted to concentrate on modernising the back kitchen. We had already made the working surface for the left-hand units with glued layers of chipboard and now we made a similar one for the sink unit on the other side. It was complicated and time-consuming to cut and fit the hole for the ceramic sink so that it fitted exactly, because the solid sink was extremely heavy to position. We put a varnished hardwood edge round both surfaces and covered them with small brown tiles. Then we decorated the walls with some ornamental tiles we'd bought as a bargain in Northwich. Fixing the sink over the tiled surface was a threat to the fingertips and putting in the tap by drilling through the ceramic surface was quite heart-stopping. We expected the whole sink to shatter any moment.

Hartford Parish Council was going to present a wood and metal garden seat to the Mornant council as a memento of the tenth anniversary and we had brought it over in kit form. We assembled it and rather than leave it incongruously in the kitchen put it outside on the front path where Elisabeth and I could sit and watch the world go by. We still needed our sweaters. Jack and I had a fire in the kitchen most evenings and always put the electric blanket on to warm the bed before we turned in at night.

Charles was at St Paradis from Paris and we saw him nearly every day in Elisabeth's kitchen, advising Paul on the Tiercé — the French horse-race betting system which relies on picking the right combination of winning numbers. Paul studied form and loved doing it, but had a lot of "near misses." The men used to joke that Michel, who picked numbers at random according to people's birthdays and only played occasionally, won quite as often as Paul.

The Lebruns' new garden was now finished, at what we presumed was great expense. The masons had made a very pleasing job of it. There was no trace of the burned house which had blighted that part of the village scene. A stone wall now ran around the old site, topped by green metal railings, the Lebruns' gable end was neatly rendered with occasional ornamental stones protruding from it to make it look old, and there was bare soil in the little garden. Sadly the rain was washing this soil down the hill into the corner of the site. It needed binding together with the roots of plants and grass.

Mme Echelle had another little dog. This one looked just like Milord but he was more of a conventional fox terrier. His name was Max and he had a curly brown and white coat with a docked tail which stuck up in the air. Max was at the bottom of the canine pecking order at the Echelle establishment and trailed round after Milord like a little brother being led into mischief. He never seemed to display any emotion. The two young dogs paid daily visits to us accompanied by Gitane. Betty popped over too, when her owners were staying in her late mistress's house. They lived in the city during the week and came over each weekend.

After the Martins had gone, we tried to work out where their woods were according to our plan of the village. However we couldn't get the cadastral numbers to marry up. We were missing part of the map which showed the land to the north of our field and eventually we decided that the simplest way of picking a suitable wood was to ask Georges if he would show us the official map held by the Mairie.

Keen for a gossip, he came round with Michel and spread the map out over the kitchen table. Both farmers, they were fascinated by the minutiae of land ownership. The French system of inheritance meant that the village arable land was divided into small plots, and some of the woods on the Martins' list were a long way from the road, in the middle of land which other residents rented or owned. Georges said that landowners were legally allowed access across other people's property, but we didn't want to fall foul of one particular neighbour and be accused of trespassing. We also preferred to get tools to the wood — and firewood off it — without a long walk. Then we saw an M-shaped piece of woodland not far from our meadow and adjoining a nearby lane. It seemed to be ideal and when we investigated later we discovered that we could see it from the house and that it featured in practically every photograph we had ever taken of our field. We had just taken it for granted.

We wrote to the Martins quoting the number of the plot and describing where it was. We asked if Jean-Luc could give us written permission to use it, just in case someone said we had no right to be there. He is a retired lawyer and replied with a typed legal document giving us and our heirs and successors permission to use the wood in perpetuity! We are very proud of it and have made several copies.

We told Georges that we were going to our twin village near Lyon at the weekend for the tenth anniversary celebrations, which fell over the French Whitsun festival. He asked us what twinning was. St Paradis' tiny commune of six hamlets with a population of two hundred was so minute that "twinning" was a concept beyond its ken.

We explained that it wasn't about "junketing on the rates" or having a free holiday at someone else's expense. The idea is to make real friends in another country and then offer reciprocal hospitality to these new friends, who share the same interests as yourself, so that national barriers are broken down. Twinning started after the war when links were made between countries who had previously been enemies (our home town of Spalding was twinned with Speyer in Germany in the '50s) so that people could meet on a human level and never feel able to demonise one another again. The concept spread. Our nearby town of Northwich is twinned with Carlow in Ireland and Dôle in France. We have made a lifelong friendship in Dôle with the parents of a lad who offered hospitality to our son Alex. Crewe, where I was a newspaper editor, is twinned with Mâcon in France and through this connection we met a young woman whom I regard as a French daughter. In Mornant, thanks to the links already established over the past ten years, Hartfordians are not tourists but members of an extended "family". When we walk down the street we are practically guaranteed to meet someone we know. Mornant is a "home from home" for us, where we have as many friends as we do in the Limousin.

The town dates back to Roman times and there are the ruins of a Roman aqueduct on the outskirts. It has a picturesque mediaeval heart which shows up as a round rabbit-warren of streets on aerial photographs. There are many modern buildings, of course, including several schools, the gendarmerie, a swimming pool, a bouledrome and a cultural centre which incorporates meeting rooms and a theatre.

Agriculture is one of the main occupations and Côteaux du Lyonnais wine is produced in the area but Mornant is near enough to Lyon to be a commuting centre, too. Our friends come from all walks of life: professionals, scientists, teachers, skilled craftsmen, businessmen and farmers. Some have lived in the area all their lives and come from long-established families, others have moved in recently to work for the major employers in Lyon. One reason why we never seriously considered buying a house in Mornant was that the proximity of the city makes property very expensive.

The countryside is quite unlike our part of the Limousin which is green and wooded with a patchwork of small pastures and ponds. Mornant is set amid the Monts du Lyonnais. On a clear day you can see Mont Blanc in the Alps across the plains covered with vineyards, cereal crops, soft fruit and orchards. The buildings have rich orange pantile roofs which stand out against the open landscape and the tall cypress trees help to lend it an almost Provençal atmosphere. Just being there gives us a thrill because it's so different from what we're used to in Hartford and St Paradis.

We set off the next day and travelled via Clermont-Ferrand — a city which has gone down in Loader family history because it is the headquarters of the giant Michelin tyre company. Chris and Linda had done a year of their electronic engineering degree course at the Michelin factory at Stoke-on-Trent, at a time when there had been massive redundancies decreed by the top management, and they always referred to Clermont-Ferrand with a shudder as "the C-F word".

In the past we had struggled to drive through the city without getting lost but this time we intended to stop at the Museum of the Resistance and Deportation. Marguerite's son Alain had been a pharmacy student at Strasbourg in occupied France and his faculty had been evacuated to Clermont-Ferrand university which was under the Vichy régime. We wanted to find out some background knowledge about what had happened there during the war.

The recently-opened museum was tucked away under a highrise development. We arrived with only three-quarters of an hour before it was due to close for lunch and were the only visitors. It was mostly devoted to the tragic story of French people who had been sent off to the concentration camps and was illustrated with ghastly photographs. There were many original documents condemning people to be deported, together with posters and press cuttings.

One section of the museum was devoted to the university. It appeared that the medical faculty under the leadership of some influential lecturers had organised a very active Resistance unit and that the Nazis had made mass arrests. More than 100 students and staff had been taken into custody in 1943 and about 80 had been sent to the camps as forced labour, including poor Alain.

A small library of specialist books was housed in a study area and it was frustrating to know that they contained a great deal of relevant information which we did not have time to examine. It is very hard to skim through a book in a foreign language looking for key words, especially if you are in a hurry. We wrote down the names and publishers of the books which seemed most appropriate, in case we were ever in a position to buy them from a bookshop. Many were academic and expensive works produced by the University of Strasbourg. A few general publications were for sale at the museum and when we left at closing time we bought a harrowing one about the history of the deportation of French Jews and French *résistantes.*

We arrived in Mornant at about 5pm, slightly earlier than we had estimated. We were staying with our old friends Chantal and Georges, who are the same age as us with grown-up children. Chantal had recently given up being a councillor but she had been one of the pioneers of the twinning and we had first met her 11 years previously when a coach party of Mornantais visited Hartford to look over their prospective "twins". She's a honey: enormously capable, practical and caring — and very highly respected in the community. Georges has a business designing and installing magnificent stone fireplaces. He trained as a plasterer but is a superbly skilled craftsman in every trade he tackles. He is a genius with stone and wood.

Early in their marriage he and Chantal bought two derelict barns on a hillside site with an idyllic view over a valley dotted with cypress trees. They dismantled them, cleaned the stone, sorted it by hand and built themselves a four-bedroomed house, with a garage, workshop and *cave* overlooking what we have always described as the most beautiful panorama in France. The inside is fitted out entirely in solid oak: doors, floors, stairs, cupboards and kitchen units. Georges even made much of the furniture in oak. The contents, fixtures and fittings must be worth a king's ransom.

We love staying with them. They both come from big families who have lived for generations in the area and the couple have a wonderful air of stability, strength and caring which is hard to find nowadays. Their roots run deep and they are quite sure of their lifestyle, culture and values. They are both excellent unaccompanied singers much in demand to perform their "party pieces" after dinners and community festivities. Neither can speak English but we get on so well that even from the earliest days we have been able to have quite complicated conversations with them, somehow or other. Being with Georges and Chantal was excellent practice for being dropped at the deep end into a St Paradis where we had no choice but to speak French.

Georges loves the countryside and is a great *chasseur*. He keeps Breton hunting dogs — who look and sound exactly like our much-loved Goldie — and these live in specially-built runs in the large garden. They also have two house dogs and it is hilarious to see all the animals let out in the garden for exercise, haring around in unalloyed glee. The dogs adore their boss and mistress and approach them with doggy grins on their faces.

The couple's one failing is that — added and abetted by us — they have a French disregard for the concept of time and it is quite usual to set out for somewhere at the time (or after!) you were supposed to have arrived. As most other people in Mornant have the same philosophy this doesn't seem to matter much!

Chantal is a childminder and since we had arrived early, she was still looking after three of her small charges until their mothers fetched them. Her own son and daughter are beautifully brought up and it's a shame that she isn't a lecturer on parenting skills. We were absorbed watching her dealing with the children, dispensing cuddles, information and a basic grounding in good manners, apparently quite effortlessly. One toddler, tackling some sophisticated morsels, was learning subconsciously from her gentle corrections and encouragement that eating was a serious business and that he mustn't play with his food. We couldn't imagine him in later life demanding a diet of junk. Not having coped with tinies for more than 20 years, I marvelled at her patience.

When the children had left, Georges arrived home from work and we had a quick meal (if such a thing exists in France!) before setting off for the first event of the weekend. We were among 24 delegates from Hartford who had made their way by car, air and train to stay in the homes of their French friends.

The celebrations started with a concert in the theatre of the new cultural centre, organised by the twinning association. The first half was performed by pupils from the secondary school choir and the orchestra of the local music school, and we were kept busy trying to spot any youngsters we knew. The second half consisted of entertainment by the professional folk group Trotwood — a French family who specialise in performing Irish and Scottish music. This was an inspired booking by the organisers because the English in the audience knew the words of most of the songs and were encouraged to join in the choruses. In no time at all a convivial and informal atmosphere had been created. It was quite surreal to listen to a French family singing with Irish and Scottish accents spiced with a slight French flavour.

Next morning we went cherry-picking in an orchard not far away owned by Georges' mother. Mornant is a fruit-growing centre and its produce is out of this world. The cherries are unlike any others I've tasted. They are fat, deep red and deliciously sweet. It's quite permitted to eat as many as you like while you're picking them. "One for you and one for the basket," said Chantal.

Then we went to see Georges and Chantal's daughter Marielle, her husband Eric and their two little girls. Both parents are primary school teachers and Marielle was on maternity leave. They live in a modern house which Georges has designed and built for them at his mother's farm on the site of an old agricultural building. As always, the workmanship is stunning and original. One of the main features of the ground floor is a woodburning stove with glass doors which is constructed between two rooms so that it can be a focal point for both. On our previous visit they had just applied for planning permission and were awaiting the verdict.

The children were entranced by some tiny chicks which had been a free gift from a feed salesman. Their parents had rigged up a makeshift incubator with a bedside lamp and a cardboard box. Our conversation was carried on to a background of chirping from the fluffy yellow creatures.

After we'd inspected the new house, Georges took us to explore a part of the farm which he was deliberately reverting to nature. He uses it to train his hunting dogs. He has built a rabbit warren on some high ground and has been busy planting gorse, brambles and other cover for rabbits all over the site and encouraging the natural vegetation. We were amused to visualise him planting brambles while we were busy digging ours up! He had brought a favourite dog with him and it was having a wonderful time following scents and disappearing into the undergrowth for minutes at a time, its presence only discernible by the shaking of an odd leaf. George encouraged it and gave it incomprehensible "hunting" instructions. It was funny to think that the dog understood his French while we didn't!

We had a formidable lunch *en famille* back at the stone house, with four generations of the family: Marielle, Eric and the children, Chantal, Georges and his mother — whom we have known for years. Chantal is a superb cook and for one of the courses she served up meat from a wild boar which Georges had shot earlier in the year and which was residing in their freezer chopped into various joints. In the past we've had delicious roast chicken that had been pecking unscathed around the farmyard the previous day. I always feel inadequate when I give her a piece of beef from Sainsburys!

While we were having our dessert, Georges and Chantal showed us photographs they had taken on a trip to Kenya the previous year with a group of fellow fireplace-specialists. They had particularly enjoyed the safari part of the holiday and we examined the menagerie of carved animals they had brought back as souvenirs.

At this point, the other English and their hosts probably visited the Maison de Pays — a 17th century building in the medieval heart of Mornant which has been converted into a museum and exhibition centre devoted to local history and culture. We've been there lots of times and it's a fascinating place. We sort of missed that bit of the programme, but it wasn't compulsory...

When lunch was over we jumped into Georges' car and dashed down to Mornant where we joined everyone else on the Place de la Liberté to enjoy an hour of music by the brass band of Taluyers-Orliénas. The musicians then led a procession to the town cemetery where national anthems were played. A slight distraction occurred when a young couple with what I suppose one should call "learning difficulties" wandered into the ceremony by accident. They stared at everyone and stood in front of the official party until someone had a quiet word in their ear and they ambled off, hand-in-hand. The new Mayor of Mornant and the chairman of Hartford Parish Council laid wreaths on the war memorial and we all stood in silence to remember the dead from both communities who had given their lives during the World Wars.

An official reception was then held at the Salle des Fêtes. The event was inaugurated by the president of the twinning committee and speeches were made by the mayor and our council chairman — who bravely dispensed with a translator and read her oration in both English and French. The two civic heads signed a charter of friendship echoing the sentiments in the one which had marked the beginning of the twinning in 1987. Gifts were exchanged: the Hartford delegation gave Mornant the bench we'd assembled at St Paradis and in return the English received a hand-crafted terracotta plaque bearing the emblems of both communities. Everyone photographed the mayor and the chairman sitting side by side on the bench — and various French friends asked where they could order one when they came to England!

Later that evening an official banquet organised by the Mornant municipal council was held in a restaurant at St Genis Laval on the outskirts of Lyon. It had white peacocks in the grounds and was built near an ancient astronomical observatory: we thought that nowadays the lights from the massive city would blank out anything worth seeing. The meal was served in an old building with an arched roof and the highlight was a cake festooned with candles to mark the "birthday" of the twinning. I sat next to the mayor and we both enjoyed our conversation. It was his first twinning weekend and he was keen to find out all about us before he and his family came over to Hartford for the twinning festival in July.

Sunday, May 18 was spent on a trip to Lyon, starting with a whirlwind guided tour of the masterpieces in the Museum of Fine Arts. Before entering, we had fun in the square outside which has jets of water spurting between the paving stones in a continuously changing aquatic "sculpture". It was a hot day and the spray from the jets was welcome. Brief snapshots in my brain remain of Egyptian sarcophagi, Greek statues, lifesize French medieval statues of the Angel Gabriel and the Virgin Mary designed to stand a certain distance apart and make eye contact, numerous

Old Masters (five minutes contemplating just one Rubens or Rembrandt would have made the whole trip worthwhile), various French Impressionists including Gauguin and even an early 20th century Russian painting.

Lunch was in the panoramic restaurant at Fourvière which gives a magnificent view of the city laid out beneath it. We gazed across the river to the famous pointed skyscraper *"Le Crayon"* (The Pencil), where my "French daughter" worked as a bilingual secretary until quite recently. The woman coach driver had a fraught time getting up to the restaurant, squeezing the bus between badly parked vehicles on the steep narrow streets with only a centimetre or so to spare on the hairpin bends. At times — let us be honest — I think we did actually nudge a car or two out of the way...

During the afternoon we had a conducted tour of the Musée Urbain dedicated to the work of French architect Tony Garnier. His prophetic designs for a modern industrial city, drawn in the early 1900s, have been reproduced as giant frescoes on the walls of blocks of apartments in the Etats Unis part of the city which he designed in the 1930s. Most of the futuristic buildings were never constructed but the designs acted as an inspiration for generations of architects to come, including Le Corbusier. It was extraordinary to see his precise architectural drawings magnified on such a vast scale. The area is not well-off but there is no graffiti or litter because the people who inhabit the apartment blocks are so proud of them. We visited one flat which had been kept as it was when Garnier designed the block. All the others have been modernised. In comparison with the poky tenements which were being put up as rented accommodation for workers in other parts of France and Europe in the same era, it was very advanced and well thought-out.

If you're ever in Lyon and you want a unique sightseeing experience, go to the Musée Urbain — especially if it's a sunny day. We bought a big poster showing nine of the murals, framed it and hung it in the study at St Paradis as a reminder of our visit.

That night we sat and talked with Chantal and Georges for hours. We hadn't been to Mornant since their daughter's marriage and they showed us the video. The bride and groom had composed most of the wedding service themselves and it included a part where Georges sang a solo. He was so emotionally affected at the time — and on seeing himself again — that it was impossible to watch the video without tears pricking our eyes. Unfortunately the posed pictures which should have been against the heavenly backdrop of the view from their terrace had been whipped up by the Mistral into a swirl of streaming chiffon and buffeted costumes.

We chatted about weddings in general and our own in particular. Georges and Chantal had been married a few months before us, in 1968, and we encouraged them to show us their photographs, promising to reciprocate when they came to stay with us in England next time. It was so nostalgic — both of us had worn very similar styles of wedding dress which were in fashion at the time. The pair looked so young at the altar but they hadn't changed much. Almost fifty, Chantal still wore her auburn hair long and straight, and she had kept her youthful figure. From a few paces she would have passed for thirty. Georges was wiry, fit and handsome. They both had a very special twinkle in their eyes. That they were such youthful-looking grandparents really didn't seem fair. Jack and I — well, we'd gone to seed a bit. His "chest" had slipped to somewhere around his waist and mine had filled out in a matronly manner to match my hips. While Chantal could probably still have squeezed into her wedding dress, mine was size 12 and I was now size 18 — so there wasn't any chance of that.

We went to bed in the small hours and got up early to have a breakfast meeting with the chairman of the twinning association and a few key people to finalise details of the visit by the Mornantais to Hartford in two months' time. Lots of things were sorted out but one major catastrophe was averted. A group of cyclists from the Mornant cycle touring club had arranged to ride to Hartford. They had planned their journey with the aid of two Michelin maps — one of France and the other of England. The itinerary was sorted out down to the last kilometre. They had allowed one day to cycle from Portsmouth to Hartford, a distance of about 250 miles by non-major roads. We were horrified. It took five hours in the car on motorways and dual carriageways.

"It's only about 200 kilometres," said their leader. "It says so on the map."

We looked at the maps. The French one was calibrated in kilometres and the English one in miles. They hadn't noticed the difference.

We recommended that they should stop around Ludlow, to give themselves time for a good night's sleep and a fairly leisurely trip up to Hartford. They changed their departure plans to fit in with the new timetable. Goodness knows what would have happened if we hadn't had the meeting.

We left Mornant well after 11am, knowing that it would not be long before we saw many of our "twins" again. We had decided to go home via the Roanne area where some good friends from Mornant had recently bought a farm and were going to raise organic crops and livestock. They had been staying there over the New Year, with about the same level of facilities as we had at St Paradis. We had swopped weather horror stories.

Murray is a New Zealander by birth. He speaks fluent French and had been working for a medical instrument company in Lyon we we first met him. His French wife Eliane is an English teacher of great academic ability. She and their son had stayed with us when she had accompanied a twinning exchange group from Mornant in the early 1990s and we had established an immediate rapport. Murray had been made redundant about the same time as me (there was a lot of it about!) and he had decided to go on a course to learn organic farming. They had looked around for a small farm in Eliane's home district and come up with one that fulfilled their criteria. They'd put their house in a village near Mornant on the market, had eventually sold it and were due to sign the *compromis de vente* the following day. The *acte de vente* was due in July. After they had taken possession of the farm at the end of 1997, Murray had spent as much time there as possible while Eliane and the children came over at weekends and for school holidays. Eliane had been appointed to a job at a good school in Roanne which she was to take up shortly and they were just poised to make a new start in life.

We were delighted to see them. We had exchanged long letters at least once a year — Eliane's always in such good English that they could have been written by a native English-speaker — but it had been a considerable time since we had met.

We mentioned that we had been to the Musée Urbain and started to explain what it was. Eliane stopped us with a laugh. She was currently teaching in a school nearby and was very familiar with it.

We found their farmhouse very interesting. The vernacular style was for buildings of *pisé* rather than stone. It's the same as "cob" in England — mud made from clay subsoil and liquified by the "puddling" method. It sets very hard and will last for centuries so long as it is protected from the rain. Rain had been the downfall of the *pisé* interior walls in our old burnt house.

Like us, they had a lot of work to do on the house. It was more or less unfurnished because all the good furniture was still in their house near Mornant, so they were "camping" like we had done at the beginning of our occupation of St Paradis. They were ahead of us in that they already had a kitchen with a woodburning stove and a bathroom. These would no doubt be modernised in the fullness of time but at least they existed. Two of the bedrooms were in a reasonable state and were wallpapered in a typically French way, but other rooms were very primitive. An attic over one part of the house was pretty unstable. On the plus side, they had some good farm buildings, including a cowshed with a chain conveyor belt to remove the muck. They had retained part of the land and rented out the rest. The farmer from whom they had bought the property was very kind and had helped them out when they needed work done by large-scale machinery. Murray had planted some organic crops as an experiment to see how they fared and was watering them with an irrigator. He hoped to buy some calves and rear them organically too.

Eliane's family lived nearby and were very supportive. They dropped by while we were there and we were very pleased to meet her younger brother again. He had stayed with us as a trainee pilot for Air France and we had managed to get him into the air traffic control tower at Manchester airport so that he could improve his command of English as it is spoken by pilots and air traffic controllers across the globe. He had flunked the vital exam in the subject before but passed it after this unique "work experience". We had become very attached to him and the unexpected reunion was a great pleasure.

We left Eliane and Murray in the early evening with our fingers very firmly crossed that they would make a go of their brave enterprise.

The journey back to St Paradis was eventful. We ran into a spectacular storm which blackened the sky and made the lightning more vivid. It rained so hard that at one point we had to stop because we couldn't see. As the storm gathered the mobile telephone rang. It was Alex. There had been terrible storms in Cheshire too and the dogs had gone berserk. They are terrified of thunder. Jazzy the Setter had tried to dig a hiding place in Mother's bed and had wee-ed all over it, soaking everything. What should they do? We advised him to take the mattress off and replace it with the one from the spare room. Fresh linen was in the airing cupboard. He could get the duvet cleaned at a specialist laundrette in the village where he lived and replace it in the meantime with another from a cupboard in one of the bedrooms.

We were glad to get home to St Paradis in the late evening.

Next morning Paul came round to tell us that he had been watching some men loitering round the house the previous day. He was afraid they might have been prospective burglars, casing the joint. The mystery was solved just before lunch when there was a knock at the door. It was a couple of approximately our age who introduced themselves as Virginie and Guy. Virginie explained that they had a *maison secondaire* tucked away around the corner, next to the farm owned by the uncle of our friend Georges the agricultural contractor. He had mentioned to them that we had gone to Lyon for a twinning weekend. She and her husband lived in Lyon and she wondered if we were associated with the twinning between Lyon and Birmingham. They had a group of friends staying with them, which included the honorary British Consul in Lyon, and she wondered if we would like to meet him. He had been looking for us at the house the previous day with some of their other guests. So much for our exalted burglars!

We explained that our connection was actually with Mornant

— which the couple knew — and we were pleased to accept their invitation to join them for the dessert course of their lunch, at 2pm. This is a common and sensible French custom which means that you can cater for extra guests without having to make a lot of additional food.

We were very interested to visit their house. It was set off a narrow lane at the back of Michel's farm which we had never explored on foot because it looked rather private. We had been down there once in Georges' car two years before and he had pointed out his uncle's home. Unless you knew where to look, the house belonging to Virginie and Guy was not immediately obvious from the bend on the main lane and we had never noticed it.

When we went round everyone was sitting around a table on the terrace at the back of the house. Before we joined them, Virginie and Guy showed us their garden. They were keen and knowledgeable gardeners with a passion for roses and it was beautiful. There were 80 different roses of all types! Virginie said she had inherited the house from her grandmother about 12 years previously and they had been renovating it ever since whenever they had the chance to get over from Lyon. We concluded that our visits to the village had never coincided before.

She had just started to serve the dessert when it started to rain heavily and we all scrambled inside to take up places around the kitchen table. We found we had a lot in common with the couple and their friends. They were easy to talk to and understand, and it added a new dimension to St Paradis for us. Virginie was a maths teacher in Lyon with training in chemistry — Jack's subject — and Guy was a retired plastics expert who loved working with his hands on the house or the land. He had lots of tools which Jack admired, especially an electric concrete mixer, but the big source of envy was a miniature tractor in the barn.

Eventually their friends left and we continued chatting with Guy and Virginie in the kitchen. Jack and Virginie became enmeshed in technical conversations about maths and chemistry and Guy and I let them get on with it! The encounter was a decided "hit" and they invited us round to dinner later in the week.

We came down to earth and for the next day or two continued

working again on the back kitchen. Then we went out and compared prices for a 150-litre electric water heater (*chauffe-eau*) to go in the bathroom. The next step in the master plan — some time in the future — would be to connect it to the hot tap over the ceramic sink. We got a *chauffe-eau* for a good price but it was massive and we wondered how on earth we were going to get it up the stairs between us. The box was rectangular and about 4ft 6ins long. It was easier to carry like that than if we had removed it and struggled with the white enamelled cylinder, but it still required a lot of effort to manhandle. We were very pleased that we had never got round to putting any bannisters on the ancient stairs.

By the end of the week the back kitchen was pretty respectable and could be used for storage and working surfaces. Brown carpet tiles and a rug covered the concrete floor and we were the only people who knew that the taps weren't attached to anything. We had connected the waste pipe in case someone thought everything was finished and inadvertently poured water down the sink.

When we had dinner with Guy and Virginie, they pulled out all the stops. Virginie had gone to a lot of trouble to prepare a meal where each course was a traditional Limousin dish and Guy had looked out some superb wines. We felt thoroughly spoiled. I wondered if, when we asked them back, I could pass off one of my variations on Chicken Tonight as a typical Cheshire recipe. They showed us round the house and the paintings on the walls bore witness to Virginie's skill as an artist.

Although we spoke French nearly all the time, we suspected that Virginie's English was as good as, or better than, our mastery of her language. When we got really stuck we were able to fall back on mutual Franglais which usually won the day.

Anyone who has to speak a foreign language will know that you have "good days" when everything flows and "bad days" when you have verbal constipation. We loved our old French friends at St Paradis but on bad days it was hard to have an intelligent conversation because we couldn't understand them very well. They didn't make any allowances for us by speaking slowly or not using their normal idioms. Because we felt embarrassed about our apparent stupidity, we became more and more tongue-tied, in a vicious circle of incomprehension and panic. We could understand Guy and Virginie easily, so conversation was a pleasure. The more we relaxed and went on to automatic pilot, the more we understood. We exchanged addresses and looked forward to meeting them next time we came on holiday.

On our last day we took the trailer out of the barn where it had stood since January and packed it as usual. It had seemed strange driving over without it. We wondered if the day would ever come when we wouldn't need to bring it, crammed full of tools and bits of furniture. We couldn't envisage a St Paradis home which was actually *finished*!

On the way home to England we analysed the visit. We hadn't done a great deal to the house but friendship had been the underlying theme. Meeting the Martins after writing to them for so long had cemented the relationship and we felt honoured to be counted as members of their family. We had really enjoyed being with Georges and Chantal, who were our oldest friends in Mornant, and seeing all the other people we knew so well through the twinning. It had been great to be in at the beginning of Eliane and Murray's big adventure and to be able to visualise what they were doing. With Virginie and Guy we felt we had started something that would blossom in the future.

And of course we had all the other folk at St Paradis who had befriended and supported us from the beginning. We were very lucky.

# Chapter Nine – July 1997

The twinning festival in July was a great success. As far as we knew, it was the first event of its kind to be held in this country. Our borough of Vale Royal is twinned with Rychnov-nad-Kneznou in the Czech Republic and towns and villages within the borough are linked with places in France, Germany, Eire, Poland and Hungary. Delegates from all these "twins" were invited to the festival and the various twinning committees took it in turns to entertain them all as well as hold events for their own particular partners.

In Hartford the French and their English hosts gathered at the village hall late on the Friday afternoon to renew old friendships and to wait for the arrival of the four cyclists and their driver, who were being escorted from Ludlow by members of the local cycle touring club. As principal organisers of the Hartford part of the programme, Jack and I had been most concerned to discover that the French hadn't arrived at their bed and breakfast accommodation in Ludlow by 10.30pm the previous night. We had visions of them being lost in Mid-Wales or squashed under the wheels of juggernauts. They were due at the village hall at 5pm and we were just panicking gently when they turned up at 6pm, saddle-sore but triumphant. They said the rain in France had been so awful that they had been forced to stop rather than drown in the driving water! Sadly they'd had to travel in the back-up car for a while simply to reach the ferry in time, so they had not achieved their ambition of cycling door to door. They had suffered various dramas en route to Ludlow and had faced bad weather on the way to Hartford. We took our hats off to them.

Thirty-eight adults and children came over from Mornant for the event and stayed in the homes of volunteer hosts. Most of these were connected with the twinning committee but as the numbers of French guests grew in the weeks before the festival we had to spread the net wider and some of the hosts were having their first contact with the Mornantais. We hoped this might lead to the sort of lifelong friendships that we had established.

A good proportion of the French delegation had never been to

*The medieval heart of Mornant – so unlike Hartford!*

Hartford before and we wondered how it would measure up to their expectations. Like Mornant the village dates back a long way: it's mentioned in the Domesday Book and it was on an old Roman road, but we don't have any really ancient buildings like those in the medieval heart of Mornant. I could spend all day there just admiring the architecture.

We were delighted that Chantal had been able to come on the trip but sorry that Georges was too busy to spare the time. In the recession which France was suffering, he couldn't afford to neglect his customers.

Mother chatted to Chantal in French — it was quite extraordinary that the part of her brain which governed remembering languages was quite unaffected. Sadly, she mistook our youthful looking friend with her long auburn pony-tail for a little girl and asked her every few minutes, with great concern, where her parents were. Chantal explained numerous times that she was actually a granny and didn't need to be accompanied by her mother and father.

At 8pm everyone turned up for a barn dance at Hartford High School organised by Hartford Twinning Committee as part of its contribution to the festival. In no time all the nationalities were intermixed as they tried to tackle the intricacies of English and Scottish country dancing. It was an ideal ice-breaker. After a few dances everyone was completely integrated — you didn't know if you had just trodden on a French toe or a Czech one! The folk group who were performing the music had a "caller" who demonstrated the dances but in the heat of the moment everyone except the experts forgot what they were supposed to do next and the dances often degenerated into a giggling chaos. It was quite exhausting but no one minded.

The wiry cyclists amazed us by being as animated as the rest. We couldn't imagine where their energy came from, especially when we learned that one of them had come at the last possible minute when one of the originals had pulled the ligaments in his ankle getting off his tractor. He had turned up at the send-off on crutches. According to a cutting from the Mornant local paper the club had played its "joker" and sent along the Fourth Musketeer.

Next day we went to the borough council open day where

there was an exhibition of twinning put on by all the different committees. The theme of our Hartford display was "Don't be a tourist — be a twin!". The stand depicted Mornant and included photographs and souvenirs of our own plus a display board, photographs and leaflets written in English, which had been brought over by the Mornantais. Reprints of reports about all our formal twinning events since the beginning in 1987 were available for people to take. The Carlow delegation dished out free Guinness and was very popular! The Dôle stand dispensed yellow Jura wine and little chunks of Franche-Comté cheese.

As the morning progressed I was aware that my upper lip was stinging and swelling. This had happened once before, when I was in the throes of being made redundant and had been under great strain. I had then finished the day looking like one of those African women with a plate in my lip. The fact that I was at a party at the time had added to my embarrassment. Afterwards the doctor said I should always carry some antihistamine with me, in case it happened again. After a few months I had forgotten his advice. Now I couldn't believe it was ballooning up at such an inconvenient time. The run-up to the festival — and dealing with Mother — had been hard work and worrying, but I didn't think I had been that stressed out. I accepted the problem in the spirit of a John Steinbeck libation to the gods for the success of the weekend— I was far too busy to let it spoil things. Jack covered for me on the stand and I slipped into the town to buy some antihistamine tablets.

After lunch and speeches, we went over to a nearby community arts centre where Hartford had staged an exhibition of watercolours and oils by two artists from the Mornant region. I was distraught when one of the staff took me into a corner and said: "You've got 32 pictures on your list and we can only find 31."

The pictures had been brought over personally by the chairman of the Mornant twinning committee, who had entrusted them to us a couple of days before. I had brought them to the arts centre the previous day for hanging. The gallery was being given a last-minute lick of paint and I'd had to leave them piled against the wall. The building had been full of workmen and anyone could have walked out with a painting tucked under their arm.

Each carried a high price tag and I had thoughts of claiming on the insurance or simply pretending to the artist back in France that Jack and I had bought the missing picture and stumping up about £300 out of our own pocket. The problem nagged away constantly at the back of my mind, like toothache. Hoping against hope that something would happen to rescue me from the predicament, I didn't tell the Mornant chairman and suffered in silence.

We then went over to the bowls club for an afternoon of fun in the sunshine at a leisurely pace. The event included a match featuring many of the "twins" and the official opening of the club's new pavilion. After a filling lunch, we happily indulged in strawberry scones with cream. There were some good *boules* players in the various French contingents and they played with enthusiasm if little understanding of the rules of crown green bowls. Smartly dressed women delegates in stilettos were encouraged to take their shoes off. Once again, everyone mucked in and it was heartwarming to see teams made up of English teenagers, Czech officials and French councillors, with no language in common, communicating with smiles and gestures.

In the evening 24 French guests and 20 Hartford hosts attended a dinner limited to 140 people held at the college of further education in the village, to mark its centenary. Those Hartford guests and hosts who were unable to take part enjoyed a buffet supper at the home of one of the host families and then went on to the pub, where the local cycling club presented an engraved plaque to their new Mornant friends and agreed to visit France the following year to ride with them in the mountains.

I had been taking the antihistamines all day and had cut right down on my alcohol consumption, as decreed on the packet. My lip had not got any bigger but I was very conscious of it. In the morning when I woke up, the swelling had gone down but there was a big blister. Then I remembered. I had taken a sip of a scalding cup of coffee after we had put up the Mornant display and had then added a lot of milk to cool it down. The incident had completely slipped my mind. I wasn't coming out in some sort of hysterical reaction to stress — I had simply burnt myself. I thought with chagrin of all the wine I'd turned down the previous day.

Later in the morning we all went to the Mayor's open day at the civic hall, where the twin delegates and their hosts enjoyed a lunch in the company of town mayors and parish council chairmen from all over the borough. We said goodbye to the cyclists who were sensibly going home by car. Their visit had added a very special dimension to the affair.

It was at the end of this event that I plucked up courage to tell the chairman of the French twinning committee that one of his precious pictures either had been pinched or had disappeared into thin air. As a true coward I had been dreading breaking the news. I was just about to say that I would pay for the painting when he stopped me.

"Don't you remember me telling you on Thursday that I hadn't been able to get one of the pictures in the car and that the list I had faxed to you was wrong?" he asked. "I gave you an amended list."

I was so relieved that I just smothered him with a big hug and a kiss. I vaguely recalled being given a second list when we rushed to unload the pictures in the rain but I hadn't registered why and I certainly hadn't noticed that it was different from the first. What a fool! I felt as though a great burden had been lifted from my shoulders and started to enjoy myself at last.

We took it easy in the afternoon and then in the evening we had our own reception for the Mornantais at the village hall. We exchanged gifts: we gave them a bronze plaque to hang in the mairie and they presented us with a tapestry depicting Mornant which had been made by four of the women guests. All the French families and their English hosts were given souvenir certificates I'd designed marking the festival and the tenth anniversary of the twinning. In his speech, the Mornant twinning committee chairman teased me about the elusive painting.

On the Monday morning some of our guests went to Chatsworth or Quarry Bank Mill with their hosts while others came with us to one of the local primary schools. The difference in the style of teaching made a big impression. The adults marvelled at how industriously the children worked while their teachers were busy dealing with us all and one child remarked: "Mummy — these teachers don't shout!" The mayor's young son was in a class which corresponded with pupils at the school. However it was his 18-month-old daughter who stole the show. In a class of seven year-olds, she pulled up one of the tiny chairs, put it at a table and proceeded to make herself quite at home. She refused to go when it was time to move on and only budged when all the visitors left the room and her mother hid behind the door. Thinking she had been left on her own, the child gave a squeak of panic and rushed out, straight into her waiting mother's arms.

Most of the festival delegates returned to their respective countries during the Monday but the chief executive of the Czech region stayed on with his family for a short holiday. We invited them for dinner later during the week.

St Paradis had been far from our minds over the previous hectic days.

During conversation we said that we were determined to go to the Czech Republic one day in order to visit Therezin, the site of the concentration camp where Alain had died, and pay our personal respects to his memory.

"My father was at Auschwitz and he was liberated from Therezin!" said the chief executive. "I go on a pilgrimage every year. My best friend is in charge of the museum there. Let us know when you want to come over."

My spine tingled in the familiar way. "I hand you over to the living," Marguerite had said...

*The back kitchen was given over to utility-room functions*

# Chapter Ten – August 1997

We arrived at St Paradis on August 21, in the middle of what seemed like a universal heatwave. Everyone was talking about global warming. Jack had been enduring temperatures in the mid 30°Cs in his non-airconditioned office at Runcorn and I was glad that my own shady workroom in our extension hardly ever caught the sun. I was enormously relieved to have been made redundant, for the heat in our upstairs editorial office at Crewe — which had large plate-glass windows — had been unbearable in previous years and I dreaded to think how my former colleagues were coping. It would have polished me off.

Mother was reasonably settled into a routine of going to the hospital psycho-geriatric unit on Tuesdays and Thursdays, and to the local authority day centre on Fridays. I had to organise all my work to fit into the precious hours when I didn't feel immediately responsible for her. From time to time she would dig in her heels and try to get out of going to the units but I hardened my heart, bundled her into the car and took her anyway. Usually by the time she arrived, she had forgotten all about any early-morning objections. We had left her in the care of my aunt, who also had to contend with four dogs. Our dear 17-year-old Irish Setter had been put to sleep the previous Christmas when life had become too irksome for her. She had been blind, deaf and doubly incontinent. That left the younger Setter, Jazz, the cross-bred labrador/sheepdog, Sally and her two offspring, Goldie and Ziggy. My aunt had been living with us almost full-time since the end of February but Goldie had only recently decided that he didn't have to bark at her every morning. He was very nervous and protective of me, and had embarrassed me hugely earlier in the year by nipping one of my male customers on the backside.

The month before, Alex and Michelle had bought an architect-designed 1960s bungalow in a village about five miles away from Hartford. It had been cleverly laid out and the builders had used the latest Sixties materials, which seemed very dated to Alex and his wife but quite modern to us. The kitchen had expensive Wrighton base units and cupboards with shiny navy blue doors and white drawers. I adored them. When we were first married in 1969 I would have killed for a kitchen like that. The youngsters hated it. We reached a compromise: we would have the old units and they could install new ones which accorded with their 1990s sensibilities. The Wrighton units were too well-built to take apart so we crammed them into the trailer to take to France. They were sufficiently out of fashion to fit in well with the ambience of the big farmhouse kitchen at St Paradis, where I needed working surfaces and storage associated with cooking. The back kitchen had been given over to utility-room type functions like washing, clothes drying and food preparation. It also doubled as a bathroom. Now we didn't have to wash ourselves in the sink by the front door or a plastic bowl in the bedroom. After our work in May the room now looked really attractive and it was hard to remember the dingy dark place whose shutters had been knitted together with ivy and brambles three years earlier.

We were looking forward to doing some more entertaining during this stay at St Paradis. My French cousin Annette (Vivienne's sister) was due to visit for the first time, and Roger and Eileen were coming too as part of another Provence holiday.

When we set off we noted that the trailer wasn't towing as well as usual. We could feel it snatching. It was very heavily laden with the kitchen units and our old lawnmower, which Jack hoped would come into its own to tackle the grass after he had first tamed it with the brushcutter. The traffic was awful for mile upon mile and we were diverted off the M40 because of an accident, which added another half an hour to the trip. We didn't arrive at Portsmouth until 10pm — half an hour before the boat was due to leave. To cap everything, Jack's worst fears were realised when we drove up the ramp to get on to the top deck of the ferry. Every single time we tackled it with a heavy trailer, he was in suspense. The car got so far up the steep slope and then failed to make any further progress. The ramp was wet with spilt oil or sea water and we were embarrassingly stuck with the wheels spinning and our trailer full of weighty Wrighton units dragging us back. As the crew began to realise they might have a problem on their hands Jack made a final desperate effort and the faithful Peugeot crawled crabwise up the incline. We were faint with relief.

The journey to Portsmouth had been a sweaty nightmare and the drive through France was even hotter. The thermometer in the car registered 38°C inside and 34°C outside, which was far too sticky for comfort. We stopped as usual at Orléans where I treated myself to a fountain pen for a fraction of what I would have paid in England. It was the *rentrée,* when the all shops were full of "back to school" bargains and the French surfaced from the heady delights of their August holiday to the realities of working life. We paused frequently in roadside *aires* for a drink of Orangina, a trip to the loo and a rest.

It seemed only right and proper that "Test Match Special" was keeping us company on the radio.

The house at St Paradis was blissfully cool. The massive granite walls were perfect insulation. Paul had opened all the windows but had closed the louvred metal shutters to keep out the heat. We broke all the rules of living in a hot country by folding back the shutters too. The house never seemed to emerge from its slumbers and start to live again until we had filled the rooms with sunshine. It was as though it went into hibernation between our visits. As usual there were lots of fine cobwebs between the beams and above the doors, and a thin layer of dust and grit was scattered everywhere. It appeared to accumulate more during the summer than the winter. The beamed ceilings were beautiful, and nothing would induce us to change them, but they did allow dust to fall through the gaps between the floorboards and on to everything below. The dirt was noticeably less in the three upstairs rooms which had boxed-in ceilings. In the very early days, wisps of straw would work their way through to our bedroom from the attic and lie incongruously on the duvet cover, but since we had swept the floors up there this happened less often.

Paul saw us arrive and helped Jack to carry in the kitchen units. He too thought they were the height of modernity and merited an *"Ooh, la la!"*

When we had unpacked the trailer and most of our boxes and bags, we went over to join Paul and Elisabeth on the terrace at the back of their house. Hugo and Hannah were there. They had at last found a house which they liked in a nearby village. They were in the fraught throes of buying it and selling their own home in

Holland. In the meantime their vendor was allowing them to do some work in the garden. The house itself was still occupied by a tenant, so they were staying with Elisabeth. The couple hoped all the transactions would be done in time for them to move in during October. We were delighted. We liked them very much and looked forward to seeing a lot more of them in the future.

We gathered that Paul had expected us the previous day. I had obviously not made it clear in my letter to them both that we were leaving England on the 20th and not arriving on that date. He had put our "lateness" down to the fact that there had been a big fire at Calais the day before. We told him that we had heard on the radio coming down about a terrible explosion in a grain depot at Bordeaux where many people had been killed.

Generous as ever, he pressed us to take some ham and butter as contributions towards our supper. We ate them with bread and cheese we had bought at Orléans and then went to bed early. With real sensual pleasure I used a fountain pen for the first time for years and wrote in my diary: "It's indescribably wonderful to be back..."

The next day we went out to explore everywhere in detail. The front of the house was magnificent: the red, pink, orange and yellow flowers which Paul had lovingly planted spilled out of his stone flowerbeds on to the path in a blaze of colour. The vine which grew across the facade was heavy with dessert grapes. We had never seen the house looking so attractive. Round the back, the cowpats in the field showed that, as always, Georges had been using the pasture right up until we arrived. The electric fence was still in place, but turned off. Paul had planted a stand of magnificent sunflowers, flanked by haricot beans, pumpkins and brightly coloured flowers, in the garden area just outside the back door. He had weeded the remaining soil, which was usually covered with grass, nettles and thistles, and raked it into a neat flat terrace. We knew from experience how difficult and back-breaking a task that was — and he had done it in temperatures sweltering enough to make the fittest young man wilt. The fig tree which Roger and Eileen had put in by the henhouse was going strong but the hydrangea at the front, which the Martins had given us in May, was suffering in the heat.

We went to the capital of the *département* to pay money into the bank and do our food shopping. After lunch we popped over to see Paul and Elisabeth and were introduced to the daughter and son-in-law of M and Mme Lebrun, who had come to stay with them for a short holiday. We were also invited to Elisabeth's birthday celebrations the following evening. We were sorry that we had not known in time to buy her a nice present in the big town. We went to see what Stoc had to offer and settled for a water carafe which was useful but not very imaginative.

Then Jack turned to me.

"I suppose you want to put the kitchen units in place?" he asked.

"Yes, please!" I replied, idly thinking that it would take an hour at the most to remove the fish tank stand (which we used as a working surface), the big oak desk (which had been too wide to make it up the stairs and had been left beside the cooker), the freezer and the gas cooker; then put the new units against the wall and replace the cooker and freezer.

"We've got to do all the electrical wiring for the house first," said Jack. "It needs to go in ducting along the wall above the new units and behind a tiled surface at the back of the units. There's no point in putting them in and taking them out again another day."

As a master of the bodge and make-do school of DIY, I could see every point in just shoving the units out of the way against the wall and being able to use them in about an hour's time. But I hadn't been married to a patient perfectionist for nearly 30 years without knowing that I wouldn't get away with it. The new units stayed in the salon and all the other stuff, including the *batterie de cuisine*, was piled into the centre of the kitchen so that Jack could run cables round the room. Instead of having transient apple-pie order as I had envisaged, we were to be in a state of chaos for the next week or so.

The weather was so hot that after Jack had cut the grass we put the picnic table and chairs outside permanently by the sunflowers and ate all our meals *al fresco*. The gas cooker was just about accessible at the bottom of the staircase and it didn't matter that the kitchen table was invisible under a covering of tools, cable drums, saucepans and cooking pots. At least we could use the back kitchen to get the food washed and ready to cook.

While Jack did unknown electrical wizardry next day, I spent my time putting white undercoat and emulsion on the area under the staircase by the back door. We were sure that the house had undergone many transformations over time and were certain that the back wall was the oldest in the building, perhaps going back to a small house which had formed the core of the bigger one. The back door frame, in cut stone blocks, looked as though it had come out of a medieval monastery. The back door itself, which opened outwards, was made from oak planks that had shrunk with time and there were gaps between the boards. During our first winter visit in 1994 — purely from instincts of self-preservation — we had covered it with bubble-wrap plastic sheet to keep out the draughts. In cold weather we also hung a heavy curtain over it backed with a thick blanket. One day Jack intended to make a new door to the same design, using the hand-forged hinges and fastener from the original and ancient seasoned oak planks which we had found on the premises.

The wooden stairs led out of the kitchen, turned at right angles across what appeared to have been a blocked-up door into the salon and slanted over the top corner of the back door. All this made us believe they were an after-thought which had perhaps replaced a big wooden ladder. Two old long-handled axes, which we took to be fire-axes, fitted into special holders on the side of the staircase ready for use in an emergency.

This area was separated from the main kitchen by a door in a wooden partition wall. The 'kitchen side' had always been painted brown (and we had repainted it in the same colour) but the 'stairs side' was unpainted and crude. The red brick wall to the right of the stairs was similarly unfinished, as though the builders had thought it really didn't count for anything. It wasn't even plastered. We kept the plastic dustbin under the stairs and didn't investigate the storage area there too closely. When we'd first cleaned out the house, Chris had found a mummified rat tucked away in a nest of old shredded wallpaper. All these factors combined to make the area feel dark and spooky, and much dirtier than it actually was. I was determined that there should be no parts of the house which made my flesh creep and so I decided to decorate what I could, to give it a bright and clean atmosphere. When it was finished the brick wall would be matt white and the door and partition grey gloss, matching the shutters and paint on the outside of the house. As part of his electrical work, Jack was going to put a light in there, too.

In the short term there wasn't much we could do about the floor. It was a museum piece — simply the soil and granite on which the house stood, crudely levelled off but uneven enough to threaten a twisted ankle if you didn't look exactly where you were going. I wasn't sentimental about it and would have covered it with concrete at the drop of a hat (someone else's hat, mind you). But Jack thought the exposed granite was so unusual that we should leave it. Marguerite hadn't given me any messages either way, but she had been a practical farmer's wife and I didn't reckon she would vote for dirt and discomfort. At some time in the past, her family had concreted the kitchen and back kitchen floors which had presumably once been rock and earth, too. I wondered why they hadn't finished the job.

In the early evening we went over to Elisabeth's birthday party. The weather was glorious and we sat outside at a table shielded with sun parasols. Hugo was a keen cook and had made some delicious food. Lots of people were there including Robert and Cécile, who were holidaying in their *maison secondaire*. Their dog behaved itself. As the evening drew in, Elisabeth's son Vincent arrived hot-foot from a Techno 'rave' at the city. He drove into the village with his ghetto blaster at full volume, the treble notes dying in the summer air and only the *choom, choom, choom* of the bass carrying across to us.

"There's something wrong with his engine," said we decidedly un-hip English souls, who cruise France to the strains of Dire Straits (and Geoffrey Boycott). We hadn't recognised it as music.

Seeing Vincent still on a high from an exhilarating X-rated weekend, busily demonstrating fire-eating on his mother's lawn, made me feel like Methuselah's wife. He's only seven years younger than me...

We sat out all evening in short sleeves and no one had even put on a pullover when it was time to go just after midnight. Jack and I had a fascinating conversation with Hugo and Hannah about senile dementia and memory loss. They knew a lot about the subject. Hugo explained that it was as though the attention span was a circle. You thought: "I must talk about X and Y" and you'd do it quite sensibly for a minute or two until you forgot you'd said it. Then the brain would get into gear again and say: "Aha! I must talk about X and Y" and so on, *ad infinitum*. The theory certainly fitted in with our own experiences of 'circular' conversations with Mother, who would cover the same subject for hours on end — then do the same with a different topic the next day.

The following morning I put another coat of white emulsion on the wall and grey gloss on the woodwork. I was delighted. The creepy area was transformed. It was slightly sad to see how ordinary it was when the spooks had been driven away, though I still hesitated about poking around where the rat's nest had been without putting on some protective clothing. That would come, I hoped, when I had finally persuaded Jack to put some self-levelling concrete down over the primitive floor.

I spent the rest of the day helping Jack with the wiring. French houses are wired up according to totally different principles from English ones and it's folly to think that you can wire something English-fashion and hope no one notices. The concept of a ring-main does not exist. Each light and socket is wired back to the fusebox — which makes for a vast number of individual wires. There's a story, perhaps apocryphal, about a French person who unknowingly bought a house which had been renovated by an English DIY fan. He asked an electrician to do a job and the chap electrocuted himself because the wiring did not behave as he expected it to.

Jack has wired our house in textbook French fashion, probably far more meticulously than a French electrician — who, like tradesmen everywhere, will always cut a corner given the chance! However, he feels that he has then covered himself if there is ever any query. I should add here that the pre-war French electrical installation we inherited was utterly lethal — cloth covered aluminium wires running inside wooden conduits held in place with nails often driven to within a hairsbreadth of the live wires inside.

The problem was that we had bought the biggest white plastic ducting possible but we still had an enormous number of wires to feed down it from all over the house. They appeared through a handily-placed hole drilled through the upstairs landing floorboards at the back of the wooden steps leading to the attic. My job was to pull the wires through the hole and then take them back to the fusebox on the far side of the kitchen so that Jack could cut off the right length. With each set of wires it became increasingly difficult to thread new ones through the hole. We left the front door wide open to let in the sunshine and to enable us to be friendly to passing neighbours.

And pass they did — especially M Lebrun's relations. They seemed to be having a family gathering and they were quite numerous. We felt very self-conscious that we should be in such a mess the first time they met us. We were quite happy to be grubby 'scruffs' in bizarre working clothing when we were with our village neighbours — after all, the farmers and other rural residents dressed for doing dirty work and we simply fitted in. But it didn't seem right to look like this in front of fellow holidaymakers who were much more neatly and conventionally attired. At one point M Lebrun's son-in-law delighted us by driving up in a 1940s Maigret-style black Citroën which was obviously a much-loved collector's item, only taken out for occasional special excursions. He parked it by our front door and we snatched a sneak photograph when no one was looking.

It took all day to thread the wires and then cram them into the ducting. We didn't have enough hands to keep stray bits inside the U-section plastic channel which was screwed to the wall and to manoeuvre the flat cover on at the same time. We could have done with a technically-minded tame octopus.

We lay in bed that night and listened to torrential rain pouring down — from midnight to after six o'clock in the morning. With no insulation under the tiles and only floorboards between us and the attic, the sounds of the downpour were very loud. Drops thudded into a bucket which we had placed under a small gap between the slates -- just above the bed. Water dripped down our bedroom chimney too and splashed on to the artificial flower arrangement in the fireplace. The weather had been so good that before we came to bed we had not thought to bring in the laminated cloth on the picnic table and the red flowery parasol. When we finally got up and examined them they were saturated but undamaged.

We had to go to the city to buy more DIY materials, and some food for Annette's stay. We mooched round the two main *bricolages* comparing price-tags — there was a constant price war between them and it always paid to do our research before we bought something. We thought we'd have a quick lunch and went to a burger bar in the commercial centre which we'd patronised on other occasions. We were too hungry to wait until we got back home and were tetchy from lack of sleep.

We joined a queue, packed with students and families. The customer in front was reading a newspaper and we read it surreptitiously over his shoulder. It took 20 minutes to work our way to the counter. The girl took our order and it was an age before the first instalment arrived. She put two portions of *frîtes* and one cheeseburger on a plastic tray and left them there in front of us for more than five minutes before the second cheeseburger was done. The original offerings were then stone cold. We divided up the hot cheeseburger so that we had at least half a palatable one each, then ploughed through *frîtes* which resembled hard matchsticks and bits of a burger which was as appetising as a soggy bath sponge. It had taken half an hour before we even sat down and we vowed never to go there again. Fast food, it wasn't. How could the French, usually so discerning, put up with such rotten service?

In a distinctly bad temper we did our food shopping and drove home with the car radio on. Jack was mollified because England were at least winning the Test Match

We were still reasonably respectable as we struggled to lift the oak desk into the salon. M Lebrun's son-in-law was outside, digging a large hole. When he saw my plight he took my end of the awkward dead weight — which was very welcome chivalry. He then helped Jack to put Alex's old units against the wall (temporarily, you understand)... We needed to do a quick transformation job on the kitchen so that Annette would never guess it had been in such turmoil. We took the opportunity of looking like normal human beings to make conversation with other members of the Lebrun family.

While we worked to tidy the kitchen we were intrigued to see the son-in-law driving around in a borrowed tractor. He attached a trailer and, helped by his son, started to bring in loads of stone which he dropped just by the hole, outside their posh new wall. His wife manhandled the rocks far more deftly than I could have done. We wondered what on earth they were doing but were too polite to ask.

Later we bumped into Georges dismantling the electric fence and gave him his usual litre of duty-free malt whisky. He looked after our land for free and we gave him the hay crop from it, but the field was very wet in places and we knew that he always got his tractor bogged down in spite of the small channels he had cut to ease the drainage. The hay wasn't particularly good quality and our little "harvest" was not a great bargain, so we liked to say 'thank you' in a tangible way. We had decided from the beginning that until we could reclaim the pond and landscape the meadow, we wanted our *hectare* to be used to help the community's economy — if only marginally. It would have been a travesty to have left it fallow, especially as it was the biggest field in the village.

That evening we sat outside to eat our supper from the picnic table, illuminated by a candle in a glass lantern. The nights were beginning to draw in but fortunately it was still warm. We loved listening to the chorus of frogs and watching the bats swooping and swirling in the dusk.

We had seen a display of apples from Mornant in the supermarket that day and had bought a bag for old times' sake although we had been perturbed by the way a young employee had been chucking them around as if they were stones. We tried them, raw, for dessert. Sure enough, they were badly bruised and not at their best. We were sad that our friends' efforts as growers had been negated at the other end of the commercial chain.

Then we went inside to sit on the kitchen sofa together, enjoy a glass or two of wine and listen to some records. Alex had given us his old hi-fi units (record deck, radio and tape recorder — now broken) years before and they had been installed in the kitchen since the beginning of our occupancy. In the early days we had brought over a lot of classical records for which we now possessed the CD versions, and we had always listened to those while we were working, if the BBC radio reception was poor or we didn't like the current programme. This time I had gone through our Hartford LP collection and brought our favourites on the grounds that we simply never listened to records at home any more. In comparison with CDs they were too short and the technical quality was often poor by modern standards. However in St Paradis, things like that didn't seem to matter. Marguerite had left home to get married long before gramophones were common and we doubted that her parents would have had one. To the 200-year-old farmhouse, even scratched LPs were pretty revolutionary.

We wallowed in an orgy of reminiscence which would have amused our children: Fairport Convention, Steeleye Span, the Albion Band, Maddy Prior, Joan Baez, Dire Straits, Billy Connolly, *The Secret Policeman's Ball*... All good middle-aged stuff. We were entertained well into the night, glad that the granite walls were nearly two feet thick and we could play the best tracks loudly without fear of disturbing the neighbours.

When we went to bed we only needed the duvet cover. It was far too hot to put even the thinnest quilt inside it. Our thermometer in the kitchen registered 26°C in the house and up to 40°C outside during the day. I had been stung on the leg, foot and stomach by a mosquito one night and so now we kept an insectocutor on in the bedroom while we were asleep. When we woke up in the early hours we found that it cast a pleasant blue light round the room — normally everything would have been jet-black.

The morning of Annette's arrival we worked like beavers to get everything finished. One great improvement was that Jack had fitted two more fluorescent lights in the kitchen, tucked behind the beams so that they were not apparent from the door. He was ready to put a set of spotlights above the cooker, too, to illuminate that area specifically. The extra strip lights — bringing the total to four — were an enormous improvement. The kitchen measured 18ft x 18ft at its smallest but only had one tall narrow window to let in the daylight. However attractive we laboured to make it, the cavernous room seemed dark and gloomy if the lights were switched off. When we had bought the house, there had been one strip light in there and the Martins told us they remembered the kitchen always being dark when they visited Marguerite.

When Annette arrived her car's '44' numberplates excited considerable interest in the village. Apart from Robert and Cécile's Paris plates it was rare to see ones from outside the *département* and its immediate neighbours.

We showed her round proudly and got out all our "treasures" — no visitor was spared them! We chatted for hours, as we had the year before with Vivienne and Jacques. Our supper was rather burnt because once again I had confused *jarret* with *gilet* and I'd had to maltreat it severely to make it edible in time. As I've lamented before, my recollection of beef terminology was awful when faced with similar chunks on a refrigerated counter. When would I remember that *jarret* was muscle from the animal's hock or knee and that I needed to chop it up and stew it rather than pot roast it whole? Sadly, my meat cookery at St Paradis was confined to two extremes — delicious and disastrous.

When we went to bed I could hardly sleep because my mosquito bites were so swollen and itchy. I wondered if everyone's reaction followed the same pattern, when the second and third days after the original bite were worse than the first. Something seemed to have made my body particularly susceptible to insect stings and French "woozles" seemed especially vicious. I had, of course, forgotten to bring any antihistamine to France...

The following day we took Annette sight-seeing at a pretty local town in the morning. As a nurse she knew exactly what antihistamine tablets and cream to request in the pharmacy, and I was very grateful. We went into a bookshop because she wanted to buy a magazine and I treated myself to an illustrated book about the region during the war, to add to my collection. It was called "The Dark Years — under the Bombs."

In the evening I salvaged my reputation as a cook by serving roast shoulder of lamb in textbook fashion. I did, at least, recognise that and know what to do with it.

After Annette had gone the next morning, heading west to see one of her sons, I dipped into my new book* with the aid of a dictionary. It was fascinating. I have always been interested in 19th and 20th century European history, indeed if I hadn't become a journalist accidentally I would have studied for a degree in history and ended up as an academic somewhere, busy doing research in dusty archives. In fact, writing books like "The Dark Years" would probably have been my forte.

As I read it, I was reminded that Annette's own mother, Helen, one of my mother's best friends whom I had always regarded as my aunt, had been in the Resistance in another part of the country. As an English woman married to a Frenchman, she was immensely lucky not to have been caught. The Resistance group in her town had found an ingenious way of getting information. When the German officers went to a certain barber's shop, they hung their jackets up. While they were having their hair cut, someone would secretly go through the pockets looking for lists of people about to be deported to Germany. Helen was involved with others in providing false papers to enable them to escape deportation. She hid the precious stamp used to validate the forged documents in the straw under her chickens in the hen-house. She also acted as a messenger, and had several close shaves when the Gestapo were looking for suspects. Helen must have spent the war on tenterhooks, waiting for the fatal knock on the door.

I had always admired her enormously for this. I sometimes wondered if I would have been brave enough to risk my life under the same circumstances — and knew that I wouldn't. I could probably have done the tasks required but I couldn't have coped with the consequences of being caught and interrogated. I'm an awful physical coward, I'm very ashamed to say. I think I would have cracked at the first hint of torture.

Helen's family believed that the stress had left its mark. She died from a sudden brain haemorrhage in her 40s — younger, I realised with a shock, than I now was — six or seven years after

*Les années sombres, Jean Bonnet, published July 1997, printed by Creuse Impression, 23150 Ahun

the end of the war. Mother was sure that the strain of those years was to blame.

I had tried my best to find out about the Resistance in our area of the Limousin, as part of my quest to discover the overall background to what Marguerite's son had done, I but didn't know much about what had happened in general to the ordinary civilians. I had no idea, for instance, that on June 19, 1940 after the fall of France, our peaceful little backwater had been heavily bombed by Italian and German planes. The Italians had been the main attackers because they were within easy reach of their home airfields. German planes would have had to fly a greater distance.

Our *département* had been on the escape route for hundreds of thousands of refugees from the north who were fleeing the invasion. They were blindly heading south − where, they didn't know. The columns of refugees were machine-gunned from the air and bombs were dropped on the the towns through which they passed. One photograph showed horses lying dead between the shafts of their heavily-laden carts. St Paradis had escaped unscathed but in our own little town, only two miles away, 14 people were reported to have been killed. There may have been others, people without identification papers, whose deaths were not recorded. Numerous refugees had hidden in the remains of the medieval fortifications.

In the town where we patronised the Stoc supermarket, the local newspaper of the time reported that 23 people were killed. In the face of such slaughter, the wounded were not counted.

It was the same story across the *département*. The author of the book, Jean Bonnet, had contacted every community, big or small, and reproduced their answers to his search for facts. I could imagine a busy part-time clerk in a rural *mairie* dashing off a quick response to his circular. Some gave detailed replies, others very strange ones. There were a few which just said: "St Joseph /Our Lady / St ....... protected our village." The random nature of fate became obvious. Many communities said that they were not bombed but they could hear or see nearby places being bombed or machine-gunned. Some said that the bomb craters were still there. A number replied that they remembered the influx of refugees and several noted where these people were sheltered during the raids. Church crypts were common hiding places. Others summed up dramatic stories in a few words: "Were bombed. Were machine-gunned but it's not known if a census was taken of the victims." In the face of this lack of detail it was touching to read: "Were machine-gunned. A poor dog was killed."

We saw Guy and Virginie and went round for a drink. They enthused about an exhibition by painters from the Creuse School which they had been to see, and gave us the publicity brochure. We thought we would take Roger and Eileen, as the poor souls rarely budged from the village when they came to stay with us.

We continued to work on the house and potter about in the garden. The mystery stones outside had taken shape. We discovered that the Lebrun family had decided to build a raised stone flowerbed on the bend in front of their new wall, partly to stop gravel being washed down the hill but also as a barrier to prevent anyone driving into the wall — though we had never seen anyone speeding round the corner. Most traffic went through the village at a snail's pace — except for the weekly refuse-chomping lorry which was always in a hurry to get to the next wheelie-bin.

We preferred Hugo's theory about the pile of stones. He said it was a plinth for a statue of Paul, sculpted with a big smile on its face and its hand raised in welcome as if to say: "Come and have a *peu de rouge...*"

# Chapter Eleven – August 1997

We had stuck to our resolution to go to bed early and get up at about 7.30am each day. When we woke on Sunday, August 31 Jack went downstairs first, as usual, and turned on Radio 4 for "On Your Farm" the fascinating weekly programme when farmers of all kinds are interviewed over breakfast. It wasn't being broadcast. He called out: "Something has happened — it's not the normal programme." Lying in bed, the newsreader's solemn voice muffled by the floorboards, I heard that a princess had been fatally injured in a car crash in Paris. Which one? I called to Jack for clarification. Was it Princess Anne? No, he replied, it was Princess Diana. I could hardly believe my ears. What was she doing in Paris??

I've never been a particular fan of royalty. As a young reporter I worked at King's Lynn which had Sandringham House on its patch. What the royal family did there was obviously private but whenever they were around in public we had to follow them, very politely, and write trite rubbish about what they were up to. It seemed an awful waste of time. They were only human, after all. When I asked the chief reporter why we did it, he said: "In case the Queen falls over and breaks her leg. Someone's got to record it for posterity." There was no such phenomenon as the *paparazzi* in those days. Before we were married Jack and I spent a memorable New Year's morning in 1968 building a snowman in the grounds of Sandringham with two other members of the local press, waiting for the royal party to come out of church and wave graciously at the loyal crowds. The weather was so appalling that we four constituted the only crowd!

In those days the Queen was the focal point and no one was too bothered about her offspring. Prince Charles and Princess Anne were teenagers and the others were hardly more than children. The Queen took the press attention in good part, but Prince Philip didn't and he used his position to be rude and patronising to our poor photographers who were only doing their job and could never answer back however much they wanted to. They would have been delighted to have told him that they would much

*Paul had planted flowers in front of the house and barn*

rather be at home or doing something more challenging than picturing him at a railway station.

Now that poor Diana had been killed, my journalistic instincts came to the fore. I was shocked that someone so young had died so pointlessly but I was also fascinated to find out how the radio would cover the unfolding story. Princess Diana had been pilloried in the papers only the week before for her romance with Dodi Fayed but now she was being transformed into some sort of saint. The original theory about her death was that the accident had been caused by the pursuing freelance photographers, and I thought that was a sad and moving irony. If she hadn't been tempted by an empty fairytale into making a disastrous marriage, she might have married a well-meaning Hooray Henry with a stately home and ended up doing good works in a fashionable county with a posse of pony-mad children. She would have been happy and only the local press would have heard of her.

The radio devoted the whole day to news and features about Diana and we left it on in the background while we wired up the bathroom lights. This involved putting on our boiler suits, taking up floorboards in the attic and getting very dusty.

At about lunchtime, Paul came over.

"Your queen is dead," he announced apologetically. "Would you like to see it on the television?"

We went across to look at the French news and were amazed that the producers devoted almost the entire hour-long programme to the tragic events in Paris. We had no idea that there was such a consuming interest in the princess in republican France. This was echoed in the evening bulletins too. Young people interviewed in Paris near the scene of the accident were genuinely upset. We had the strange experience of seeing French journalists talking to English people in London and having their answers dubbed into French while we lip-read what they said. The great groundswell of public grief was just beginning.

We watched the news each evening over the next day or two. Paul dismissed the wilder theories about the cause of the crash. "The driver was drunk and couldn't handle the car," he said, with the wisdom of an octogenarian.

Next day I started to paint the landing walls brilliant white. It made an enormous difference to the stairwell, which had always been dark and dreary. I took a gamble, painting directly on to limewash without treating the surface first. I knew from experience that it might lift off in places. The ancient lumpy back wall needed repointing outside and there were places where the damp had permeated the mortar to create a sort of crust. I brushed it off and kept my fingers crossed.

We decided to insulate the space between the false ceiling in the bathroom and the attic floorboards with rockwool. Once more this entailed dressing up in the boiler suits and donning masks and thick gloves. We were thus attired when there was a knock at the kitchen door. M Lebrun was there, kindly inviting us round for a drink that evening.

Later that afternoon I managed to wash my hair so that I no longer looked like a dusty and rockwoolly freak. With some make-up and a clean dress I felt like a new woman.

The Lebruns opened a bottle of champagne and thanked us for enabling them transform the old burnt house. We chatted about all sorts of things. M Lebrun said that after his graduation he had taken a job in Arras in north eastern France, not far from the Belgian border. He and his wife had lived there ever since, but still kept their *maison secondaire* in St Paradis, together with various other properties.

Then I mentioned "The Dark Years" and what I had read. We discussed the war. M Lebrun had been in Arras at the time but Mme had been staying at St Paradis on June 19, 1940. She watched the raid and heard the bombs falling on the adjacent town and the main road not far away.

They told us that Arras had suffered far more from Allied bombing than German. They had endured 19 air raids perpetrated by their own side, and their own house had been damaged. They said they much preferred British bombers to American. The British risked anti-aircraft fire to come in low and aimed their bombs at legitimate targets; the Americans stayed high up and just dropped them indiscriminately on everything. The elderly couple, understandably, seemed more anti-American than anti-German. Mr Lebrun said the ordinary German occupying forces had been quite civilised, though of course the Gestapo were another story.

Poor Arras had been in the front line during the carnage of the First World War, too. Jack and I felt lucky to be living in more peaceful times.

We spent a convivial time with them. Apart from the sale of the burnt house, we had not had a long and relaxed conversation with them before. Most of our exchanges took place in the middle of the little road we shared, when we happened to bump into one another.

Next morning we drove to spend the day with the Martins. They were wonderfully welcoming and Geneviève served a delicious lunch of traditional French cuisine. We were staggered when we saw the superb wine that Jean-Luc had opened in our honour: it was the finest we had ever tasted.

We could understand why they had reluctantly decided to sell Marguerite's house at St Paradis. In addition to the small house which they had renovated and used as their *maison secondaire*, they had also inherited a former restaurant next door, a cottage opposite and a large three-storey house nearby where Jean-Luc had been born. They had enough potential renovation work to last a lifetime! Indeed, keeping all these places weatherproof would have been a major commitment. Jean-Luc said that in the old days the town had been divided between a handful of principal landowners and his family had owned most of where we stood.

Geneviève is a keen gardener and their garden was a tribute to her skills. In a shed she had a horsedrawn vehicle which she was keeping as part of a collection of old items. We could now see why, when they had visited us, she had been so interested in the veritable museum which we had found in our attic. By rights, our treasures should have belonged to the Martins and we were very grateful that they had not taken them away before they sold the house.

In the afternoon they took us for a drive in the surrounding Forest of Mérignat, which was quite different from our neighbourhood. It had been important in Gallo-Romanic times and was real "Asterix country". We went to the village of St Goussaud, named after Gonsaldus, a seventh century hermit and saint. Its Roman name was 'Praetorium'. The community, now insignificant but once important, had grown up at the wide fork of an imperial Roman road which led from Limoges and then went either to Bourges or Chateauroux. A smaller road had also snaked through, bisecting the fork and going roughly north-south. Not far away, in the forest, were the remains of a Roman theatre and a temple. Inside the church was a very old statue of the saint himself, reminiscent of the ones of the bishop at St Paradis. At his feet was a crude wooden bull festooned with sharp needles. Apparently those wishing to get married in the following year speared the bull with a needle to make sure their prayers would be answered. At the altar end of the church was a triptych of paintings depicting a modern nativity, with a supermarket trolley for baby Jesus's crib and Joseph in jeans and trainers. A boy in the foreground played the guitar and the shepherds had woolly hats. In such an ancient setting the pictures were bizarre but still devotional. Outside we moved the car to the village centre and then walked down a footpath to a small 12th century stone tower like a miniature lighthouse, known as *La Lanterne des Morts*, which was said to have been illuminated with a candle at night to keep watch over the dead. Then we walked on through the woods and climbed up to an observatory at a height of about 700m with a panoramic view for miles around and a plan to show what was what. Sadly it also showed that a mist was rising between the hills and that it would soon be difficult to appreciate the views.

Back in the car we explored the hills and forest by road then stopped for a walk at a point where several roads intersected. An old house was being 'done up' there by an English family. It was right out in the wilds and unoccupied that day. We peeped through the grimy windows and recognised all the signs — the drums of cable and the building materials scattered about. What the Martins wanted to show us was a hand-written sign pinned to the barn door, which had amused them enormously. "No parking, please" it said. We couldn't imagine the circumstances which had led to it being put up. With miles of empty road all around, who would have parked in front of their barn — and why?

We went on to Bénévent l'Abbaye, which is on the pilgrimage

route to Compostelle. It's famous for its beautiful abbey, founded in the 11th century and dedicated to St Barthélemy, whose relics were brought to the church 900 years ago. The main door in the heavily-ornamented entrance appeared to be locked but as we approached the caretaker came out. Geneviève knew her and asked if we could have a look round. She was happy to show us and was a knowledgeable and enthusiastic guide. The abbey was magnificent but the most striking feature was an arc of tall stone columns with carved capitals, all different. They were incredibly old, almost pagan, and unlike anything I'd ever seen in an English church. Geneviève later bought us a booklet by a local doctor who has interpreted the symbols and published his conclusions. There was also a statue of St Barthélemy, the patron saint of butchers. If I recall rightly, he had a carving knife in his hand and animals at his feet. The French are not sentimental about such things. The tomb of Abbot Humbert, who founded the original priory in 1028, was in the Lady Chapel covered by a flat stone with an effigy on it. The bells of the church clock tolled while we were in there and the sound echoed round the building. When we came out we shook hands with the caretaker and then walked round the grounds. Geneviève pointed out the carved stone heads, all different, which were under the eaves of the abbey roof. The abbey stands on a hill with a view over the wooded countryside, flanked on one side by a courtyard and stone buildings where the monks lived and hospitality was traditionally offered to pilgrims. The *mairie* and a school occupy them now.

It was beginning to get dark so Geneviève drove us back to their home. After such a filling lunch none of us was especially hungry but we enjoyed eating slices of the local delicacy, a Creusoise tart (rather like a Bakewell tart) made from crushed nuts on a bed of pastry. Virginie had recently passed her grandmother's recipe on to me but it was a bit too complicated for my culinary skills. The Martins gave us two to take home, one for ourselves and one for my mother, which was very generous. They also gave us an electric fire which had belonged to Marguerite at St Paradis. The cardboard box in which it had been delivered in the 1980s was one of the few modern things we had found in the salon when we moved in! Their final act of kindness was to drive ahead of us back to the main road, which was difficult to find. When we finally arrived home it was dark and late but we'd had a marvellous day. After exchanging so many letters, it had been great fun to spend time with Jean-Luc and Geneviève and know that our friendship was real. They had certainly made us feel part of their family.

We had to come down to earth the next day. We fixed the *chauffe-eau* on to its wooden plinth in the bathroom and screwed it to a bracket on the wall. I finished painting the landing walls white and then painted the skirting boards and door frames green, as they had been originally. Jack wired up a halogen lamp to go on the back of the house to illuminate the garden. While he was fixing it on its bracket he was able to confirm how bad some of the pointing was. We mixed up some mortar in a bucket and he spent an hour or so high on the ladder filling in the worst gaps. He could get almost a bucketful into some of them. Then he cleared the undergrowth from round the oak saplings we had planted at the bottom of the field.

We were busy until 5pm when Roger and Eileen arrived, as always generously bearing lots of food.

We sat round the picnic table near the sunflowers, drinking wine and chatting. We had to be careful where we positioned the plastic chairs. If a chair-leg hit a soft patch of earth and sank, the chair was liable to tip over, depositing its occupant slowly and gracefully in a heap on the ground.

We watched the lizards scurrying up the walls of the henhouse, behind the fig tree. Then our attention was diverted to some movement nearer the ground. When we had done the drains a year before, Jack had made a rough wall of a line of large granite rocks which had been scattered over the would-be terrace area. We saw a young shrew clambering up the side of one of the stones, which was dotted with moss. The little animal was delightful. It measured about two inches long and its head was almost as big as its body. It had an elongated pointed nose with wiffly whiskers and a long tail. Its fur was grey on top with a white underbelly. As we watched, two more emerged from the cover of dead leaves under the stone, playing together like young puppies. We decided

they must all be part of the same litter. The two seemed insepara-
ble, like Ziggy and Goldie, and did everything together. The first
shrew was much more independent. He scuttled around on and
under the stone while the other two scrambled up and cuddled
together in the evening sun on a relatively flat facet of the granite.
The first one tried to join them, tucking its nose under one and
jerking it up to make a place for itself. Its sibling lost its grip on
the rock and fell off, rolling over and over, while the cuddling
companion, its equilibrium disturbed, tumbled off a second or
two later. They decided this was a good game and repeated it several times, sometimes falling off simultaneously, other times individually — always coming back for more. We could have been
watching children in a playground. They were totally unafraid of
us, and the first one scampered round our feet at one point. We
observed them, utterly entranced and laughing out loud, until
they got bored and disappeared back under the stone.

The following morning we all set off in our car to see the
"Masters of the Creuse" exhibition at Dun-le-Palestel. Jack and I
were conscious that we spent so much time working on the house,
doing routine shopping in the two local towns and going to the
big towns when we needed something special, that we only went
sight-seeing when we had visitors. An accomplished artist,
Virginie had thoroughly recommended the exhibition, as well as
suggesting that we have lunch at a restaurant in a town nearby
and then go in search of the vantage points from where the pictures had been painted.

I did some homework.

Impressionist Claude Monet was the first and most important
painter to be enchanted by the beauty of the Creuse valley. He
stayed at Fresselines, with the poet Maurice Rollinat, between
March and May 1889, in spite of cold weather, rain, and alternat-
ing sunny spells, showers and snow! He found it hard to capture
his landscapes as the light — so important to his style — changed
drastically from one day to the next, and the height of the river
rose and dropped according to the rainfall. This made him very
bad-tempered, as was evident in blistering letters he wrote to his
friends at the time. Nevertheless he worked on twenty-three

Creuse canvases, many of which are now in American collections.

Monet's work inspired others, who became known collectively as the School of the Creuse. Their leader was Armand Guillaumin, a friend of Cézanne and Pissarro, who was considered to be one of the founders of Impressionism. He won a lot of money in the National Lottery in 1891 and a couple of years later chose to come and live at Crozant on the River Creuse.

The exhibition, subtitled "The Masterpieces of the School of Crozant-Gargilesse" was staged in the Salle Apollo, a cinema which had been converted into a community arts centre at Dun-le-Palestel. It had been set up by the Association Les Amis des Peintres de l'Ecole de Crozant et de Gargilesse based at Guéret. No expense had been spared with the setting and we were impressed that a relatively small place could have designed it all so expertly. In my experience, the French are pastmasters at this sort of thing.

The organisers had included works painted before the advent of Impressionism (back to the 1830s), and ones from later genres (up to 1930), to show the contrasting ways in which artists had tackled the same subjects. Identical views cropped up again and again, especially of the ruined castle at Crozant, a watermill and certain waterfalls along the river.

The pictures had been borrowed from private collections or art galleries. The only Monet, *Les Ravins de la Creuse,* had been loaned by the Museum of Fine Art at Reims. It featured on the cover of the programme in a glorious haze of blues and purples, and we were particularly keen to see it. I love the Impressionists, but I was sadly disappointed. The painting had a tracery of cracks and the colours were more muted than in the reproduction. The application of the paint looked crude and it had no life. Jack, Roger and Eileen felt the same, but it didn't matter — some of the other works, by artists unknown to us, were very good and well worth coming to see. We wandered individually round the exhibition, enjoying the pictures and lingering in front our favourites. I noticed that Jack kept returning to the Monet, arms crossed, fingering his beard and stepping backwards and forwards. After about an hour, the inevitable lunchtime closure loomed and we left.

I remarked to him: "I was disappointed with the Monet. I thought it needed a good cleaning."

"Me too," he said. "But I thought Monet couldn't be so famous unless he was really exceptional, so I kept trying. And I found that when I got to a certain position in front of the picture, it was transformed. It was absolutely beautiful and I could see exactly why people raved about it. But if I moved out of that position it was nothing."

I was sorry that I hadn't persevered. If we ever go to Reims I'll have another try. But I still think the painting needs restoring. I'm looking at the postcard version of it as I write, which was taken from the programme, and it's mesmerisingly good — a tribute to the graphic artist who tweaked it on his computer!

We drove along to Crozant, to the restaurant recommended by Virginie. We found it easily. It was packed and through the open windows the sounds of convivial chatter and clinking cutlery filled the street. Mouth-watering smells wafted out on to the pavement. It had a special entry in the red Michelin guide for its regional menu and the waitress was in traditional costume. We spent a pleasant time there, enjoying a multi-course menu. We didn't want to eat too much because Virginie and Guy were coming for dinner that night, but it wasn't the sort of place where you could get away with only a couple of courses.

Afterwards we gave ourselves a limited time for further sightseeing before we needed to go home to prepare the evening meal. As always, we had badly miscalculated and we promised ourselves another day out in the area, another time. We couldn't visit the famous ruins at Crozant, which stand on a spectacular tongue of land where the Sedelle and Creuse rivers join, but we climbed up to get a good look at them. The next port of call was a bend where a curiously round heather-covered hill plunged down to the twinkling river, which featured in many of the exhibition's paintings. A hotel there, with a panoramic restaurant clinging to the side of a cliff overlooking the view, was surprisingly closed down. We were astonished that its proprietors couldn't make a living at a site which must be visited by most tourists in the neighbourhood.

We followed the signs to Lake Chambon which had been created as part of a hydro-electric scheme on the Creuse. We watched water-skiers and people with power boats, then photographed a dog with a red collar which was begging its boss for a ride in his boat. When he refused, it walked sadly back over a pontoon bridge to the bank where its mistress was waiting.

We stayed as long as we dared but had to hurry back home. Roger and Eileen prepared the food they had brought the day before and I concocted some other things. We all had a really enjoyable evening with Virginie and Guy, and discussed our opinions about the exhibition at Dun. They were also pleased to meet some fellow expert gardeners. The Loaders know a nettle from a nasturtium, and can brew a good compost heap, but that's about it. The Williamsons are the bee's knees when it comes to gardening.

I remember the next morning with acute embarrassment. Jack was very busy trying to complete his self-imposed tasks before we set off for home, so I took Roger and Eileen to show them the wood. I was wearing old trousers and hiking boots but they were in ordinary clothes and they declined to venture in very far. As I've said before, it's M-shaped and probably about half an acre in area. It's full of deciduous trees which were coppiced when it was properly managed by Marguerite's family, but it has now gone wild. There's a lot of undergrowth and in the summer tendrils of brambles and wild roses can grab you quite painfully. Jack had asked me to report back, so I thought I would just have a quick look where we had explored in May. The wood is bounded all the way round by a barbed wire fence and a hedge in various stages of height and thickness. I walked a short distance over thick brambles on a path which was almost impossible to identify and found myself at the edge. I thought I was retracing my steps but ended up at another edge.

"This is silly," I thought. "The exit to the lane must be over *there...*" So I clambered over the prickles and skirted the trees to where I was sure Roger and Eileen were waiting for me. I bumped into another part of the hedge and didn't even recognise where I was. So I tried again. And again. And again.

Eventually I heard Roger call out: "Are you all right?" He was mercifully close and I stumbled with enormous relief to where the voice was coming from.

"You've been half an hour," he said. "We were beginning to get worried about you."

"Not half as worried as I was!" I replied.

Jack thought it was hilarious. "That wood is only twice as big as our garden at home," he said. "How on earth could you get lost in it? It's not possible."

But it was.

I went to the market in the town with Roger and Eileen while Jack carried on with his jobs. The *foire* is only held on the 5th and the 20th of the month and is a focal point of local life, so it would have been a shame to have missed it. The market place was full of stalls (including the usual pinny vendors), selling everything from fruit and vegetables to washing-up bowls and vegetables. Eileen looked at cross-stitch patterns and I bought Jack a new (male) handbag to replace his current one which was decidedly tatty round the edges, and two bowls to enable us to feed scraps to our visiting dogs. We went to a stall where the Williamsons had bought vegetables when they were in the house on their own. The stallholder had the most amazing squeaky voice. The poor man couldn't help it but he sounded just like Minny Mouse. I didn't buy anything perishable because we were leaving for home the following day, but Roger and Eileen got a few things to use when they got down to Provence.

Virginie came along when we got back to St Paradis and asked us round later in the afternoon. Jack was still busy strimming the back, putting the lawn mower together and planting clematis cuttings we had brought from England, so we went without him. Virginie brought out a box of her own family "treasures" (she had inherited their house from her grandmother) and we had a fascinating time looking at old photographs. She hadn't known Marguerite or her father and uncle, so she wasn't able to identify them. However we did recognise quite a few of the people on the wedding photographs which had been carefully posed in front of the old *auberge* where Mme Echelle lived today. One couple were Michel and his wife. He had hardly changed in 50 years and she looked stunning in her elegant dress. She was handsome now, in her 70s, and had certainly been a beauty in her youth. The shy

Michel had done very well for himself.

In the early evening, Paul and Elisabeth came over for drinks to mark our last night in the village. Jack was making a trellis for the clematis on the kitchen floor and finished nailing it together thirty seconds before they arrived.

We all packed up the following morning. Roger and Eileen left at 10.30am for the drive south, and we turned on the radio to listen to Princess Diana's funeral. The reception was poor but we found it moving, though we weren't impressed with the mawkish "Candle in the Wind" and the strange phenomenon of people applauding during a funeral when Earl Spencer had his say. We had rather lost touch with events in England over the past two or three days and from the perspective of a foreign country, it seemed as if some of the British had gone collectively and hysterically round the bend.

Jack and I picked the pumpkins, the grapes from the vine over the front of the house and the heads of the ripe sunflowers, and put them in a box to take back to Hartford. We couldn't waste Paul's efforts.

When the trailer was packed and we were all ready to go we went to say goodbye to Paul and Elisabeth. While we were there, Mme Echelle's son rushed in and told us that there was a great bulge in one of the trailer tyres. He and Charles helped us to change the wheel and put on the spare — which of course entailed removing the cover and unpacking half the trailer to find it. When we took the wheel to a tyre fitters in Northwich they said that the weakening in the tyre wall had been caused by leaving the trailer in freezing temperatures, in the same position, when we were forced to go home without it in January. We were very pleased that the problem had happened before we set out to drive at speed on the autoroute — and after we had made two uneventful journeys with the damaged tyre.

We were discussing this as we drove along the main road to the nearest city, where we were to join the autoroute. Suddenly the car in front of us braked and went straight down into the ditch beside the road. The princess's death had dinned into us what a major offence it was not to stop and offer aid after an accident, so we stopped, along with several French cars. The driver was OK, though furious with the vehicle in front of him, which had turned sharply into a narrow lane to the right and forced him to brake on a slippery bit of road. One of the French motorists was using his mobile phone to get assistance, so we drove on, shaken. Were these things going to happen in threes? Fortunately, they didn't.

We arrived at Le Havre in plenty of time and joined the long queues on the dark quay. The port was hosting a festival of the sea and the harbour to the right of the ferry berths was full of light and sound. We left the car and went to find out what was happening, peering through the wire netting which fenced us off. In front of a large block of tiered seats, little fishing boats were 'dancing' to music played over loudspeakers and letting off fireworks from their decks. The harbour, wreathed in an orange glow, was misty with smoke from the fireworks and it was hard to see exactly what was happening. The manoeuvring seemed a bit random but it was obvious that those taking part were having the time of their lives. It also appeared to be pretty risky both for those letting off the fireworks and those on the shore. We watched a rocket snake into the air and then fall underneath a caravan left on the dockside, where its remains lay smouldering. We were pleased it hadn't landed under our car or on the trailer. Those considerations apart, we were enthralled by the spectacle and by the music. Played by a full orchestra, it was wonderfully evocative with moving choral bits, and we could hum along after we'd listened for a few minutes — but we couldn't decide what it was. Jack plumped for something by Fauré while I wondered if it was from a film score. Whatever it was, it thrilled us to the core. The display ended with a climax of bangs and rockets, everyone applauded (including the waiting ferry passengers who had watched it for free!) and the harbour went quiet and dark. It was with a sense of anticlimax that we got back into the car to await our call into the bowels of the ship. The experience had been quite magical.

*The little second-hand Godin, on the right, kept us warm for the first time: so we bought the big one to install properly later.*

# Chapter Twelve – New Year 1998

Our local papers are delivered every Wednesday morning and Jack scans through the small ads while he eats his breakfast, so that if something is advertised that we want, we stand a good chance of getting our bid in early. I'm still lazily in bed at this point.

Soon after we returned from our visit to St Paradis he was going through this ritual and called out to me: "There's a French Godin wood-burning stove in the paper and it's only £50. For that price it's worth having whatever condition it's in."

I spent a frustrating morning telephoning the advertiser's number and receiving no reply. When the sellers eventually answered I was sure they would say that the bargain stove had already been sold. It hadn't. We arranged to go and have a look that evening.

All day we envisaged a plain black rectangular stove of the kind we had seen in umpteen French *bricolages*, which would fit nicely into our 6ft 6ins wide fireplace. In a country where wood-burning stoves are as ubiquitous as coal fires used to be in England, "Godin" is as well-known a word as, say, "Baxi", is at home. After the freezing discomfort of the previous New Year at St Paradis, we were determined never to be so cold there again.

When we saw the stove, it was small and upright like a squashed cylinder. It reminded me of the black cast-iron version behind a brass fireguard which had heated my primary school-room. It also brought to mind countless war films of Nissen huts filled with shivering servicemen huddled around such stoves. This one, however, was pretty rather than just functional. Its ornate metal lid, feet and front-opening door were coated in shiny brown enamel. The body was steel sheet — and rather rusty. We were told it would take coke or wood. It wasn't at all what we had in mind and we doubted if it would make much impression on the vast French kitchen, but it was only £50 and we thought that Fate must have directed us to find the only Godin *poële* in Cheshire. We bought it and after a considerable struggle, and the roping-in of an innocent decorator working for the vendors, we managed to manhandle it into the back of the Peugeot. Alex was summoned to help get it out again. It was very heavy and awkward.

Jack couldn't resist playing with it. His pyromaniac instincts were stirred and he just had to make sure it worked. That weekend he rigged up a short makeshift chimney, put the stove in the middle of the lawn and lit it with some bits of wood. The ensuing fire glowed a satisfying red through the dirty glass in the door, smoke came out of the "chimney" and we were in business. Goodness knows what the neighbours thought. We had a long length of flexible stainless steel flue left over from installing Jack's mother's central heating next door and decided to take that to St Paradis to direct the smoke up the chimney and create a draught.

During September and October I was busy putting the finishing touches to our first book about St Paradis, "A Bull by the Back Door". I had to have the covers reprinted at the last moment which stretched my little publishing business's budget almost to breaking point. I was filled with misgivings. The week before the launch party I had a constant sick feeling in the pit of my stomach. What if there was a ghastly mistake lurking in the text? What if no one liked it?

I felt in need of a new image and had my curly perm cut out. The hairdresser cropped my hair really short and tinted it with auburn highlights. If I didn't feel bright inside, I was going to look bright outside.

Jack went down with 'flu during the launch party. He had prepared a good speech but felt so ill he could barely see his notes. He didn't tell me until afterwards, when everything else had gone perfectly. The books sold well, disappearing quickly from their boxes in the office, and I did my first reprint after two months.

Auntie was still with us for a large proportion of the time, looking after Mother's immediate needs and keeping her company. She was wonderful, especially in the mornings when Mother couldn't decide what to wear. Always elegant, she had lots of attractive clothes but she had now got to the point where she couldn't remember what they were. "I haven't got anything to put on!" was the daily *cri de coeur*. It was irritating but very understandable. I recalled how I had regular nightmares before our marriage when I would be faced with agonies of indecision and a wardrobe full of the wrong clothes. In my dream I would always turn up at the wedding in something wildly unsuitable — only realising its unsuitability as I walked down the aisle and it was too late to change. At that point I invariably woke up in a cold sweat of panic. I was sure that my poor mother felt like this all the time, in spite of the fact that to everyone else she looked quite normally dressed.

The Martins had set us an interesting task for our New Year trip to St Paradis. Jean-Luc had some deeds which showed that in the 1880s our house had been exchanged, within the family, for another in the village. It had not, as we had thought, belonged to Marguerite's direct forebears for generations. We were all very keen to work out which had been her grandparents' original home. We had the descriptions of the two properties in the legal documents for the swap. The description of our house corresponded almost exactly to its present state, and we needed to follow up the clues about the other house and its associated land to decide if it was still there.

We left England on Sunday, December 28 — half an hour later than we had intended because our last-minute routine check to see if the trailer lights were working had produced the wrong answer — they weren't. After all the packing and preparations, it was quite an anticlimax.

The traffic on the M6 was appalling. We had hoped that a Sunday afternoon would be a good day to travel, but so had the rest of the population, obviously. Three lanes moved abreast at 20mph or less between Holmes Chapel and the RAC Control Centre at Birmingham. From that point there were no more jams but the traffic was heavier than we had ever seen it. We were pleased to have our minds taken off the tedious journey by the music we were able to play on a portable CD player which the boys had given Jack for Christmas. He had fitted it between the front seats of the car and we had brought along a box of our favourite CDs.

The ferry wasn't busy. We were on the bottom deck with all the lorries and had a great deal of space to ourselves for the first time. We could actually get out of the car doors without squeezing through a tiny gap and wishing we were anorexic. Our cabin was quite posh — we were on C deck, right at the front and facing forwards so we could see where we were sailing. Or we could have done if it hadn't been pitch dark.

Jack slept well but I was cold. My duvet didn't seem wide enough or long enough. There were always draughts at the front or back, top or bottom, and they kept waking me up. I was annoyed because I was pretty whacked and needed a holiday. I couldn't sleep properly at home because I always had one ear open for Mother, a legacy of the days when she had prowled around looking for the "men". She hadn't done it for months but my brain wouldn't accept that: it ticked away on automatic pilot all the time and just wouldn't switch off.

The journey seemed doomed. I had been wearing bi-focals for 18 months but I still had my old glasses as spares. I thought I would have a rest from the bi-focals and put on the "long distance" ones as an experiment. I would be looking out of the car windscreen for 360 miles, I reasoned, I didn't need to see anything close up. This was fine until we came to the toll at the Pont de Tancarville about half an hour later, at 6.30am. I was uncoordinated from lack of sleep as well as visually impaired. I put my arm out of the window to insert 15FF in the automatic basket of the toll booth, misjudged it because it was too close to see properly and dropped the 10FF coin. Embarrassed I had to get out of the car and try to find it. I asked Jack to reverse the car so I could see if it was underneath but had no luck. A woman attendant came over to see what the silly English were doing. I explained, saying I'd already put 5FF in the machine. I then put in 10FF more but the barrier wouldn't lift. I had obviously confused it. She remonstrated with me and said I hadn't paid enough. She wanted another 5FF. I was damned if I was going to feed any more hard-earned cash into the thing. I was so annoyed that I gibbered back hysterically in dreadful French and she eventually shrugged her shoulders and let us through.

We stopped at Orléans as usual. I wanted to buy a fabric *jeté* to throw over a little black sofa we had been given by some friends for the study at St Paradis. It had a mark on the upholstery where someone had squashed a pizza and I wanted to disguise that as well as make it a lighter colour. I knew *jetés* were common in France and had set my heart on getting one. I had allocated the cash from my Christmas present money. Just what I wanted was pictured in the booklet advertising the Orléans hypermarket's current 'linen event' sale. There was no sign of it anywhere in the enormous shop, which was very frustrating. I combed the entire place with no success and wasted a lot of time.

On the road again, we were talking about this failure and discussing how hungry we were. I collected a ticket at the autoroute toll-booth and we set off towards Clermont-Ferrand, looking out for the *aire* where we usually stop to eat a picnic lunch. We couldn't find it, and we noticed that the roadside signs were in a different style from what we remembered. It seemed as if the autoroute had been taken over by a new company. It also had unfamiliar place-names on it. We were very puzzled. I looked at the map. We were heading off on the wrong road... There are two autoroutes which join at Orléans and we had been so busy chatting that we had failed to turn off on to the A71. We were on the A10. Instead of going towards Clermont Ferrand we were on our way to Bordeaux. After three and a half years of journeying to St Paradis on the same route we had long ceased to navigate by the road signs. We knew exactly where we were going. Or so we had always believed...

We had missed the first junction off and the next was near Blois, more than 15 miles away. We were going to have to drive a total of 31 miles simply to turn round. We had resigned ourselves to wasting a lot of time and diesel just getting back to where we had started from, when the new CD player stopped. We poked it and swore at it but nothing happened. It would play for a few seconds and then cut out. It never worked again (we had to take it back to the shop) and all our plans for listening to CDs in transit and at the house were foiled. The only good thing about the episode was that we did a naughty U-turn in a slip-road system near Blois and managed to get back on to the autoroute without leaving it and paying a toll. We diddled the French motorway system out of 62 miles of inadvertent road use, which made us feel marginally better.

Heading in the right direction on the A71 we went suddenly from bright wintry sunshine into what appeared to be thick smoke. We drove along slowly in this enveloping blanket for some miles, not able to see into the distance but aware that the pseudo-fog finished not far above our heads. It was a very bizarre phenomenon.

We were struck by the mildness of the weather, especially in contrast with 1996-7, when at an exactly comparable time we had driven through snow and got stuck on sheet ice.

We arrived at St Paradis at 6pm. We unpacked the car and trailer in the dark and were pleasantly surprised to find that we had no problems manoeuvring the little Godin into the kitchen. We had expected to ask for reinforcements in the form of Michel or Paul.

When we did our initial check of the house we saw that it appeared to have been infested with flies. They were lying dead or dying everywhere, especially by the windows and on the window ledges. It was revolting. We recalled a similar occurrence at Jack's half-sister's home on Dartmoor one warm February, when our bedroom had been filled with hundreds of dying flies which had come out of hibernation too early and did not have the strength, or the food, to survive.

Among the post and circulars on the kitchen table was a copy of the commune's annual newsletter — the third that had been produced. We looked forward to reading it properly when we had time. I had done a similar monthly one for Hartford for more than 10 years when the boys were small and I was working from home.

I switched on the electric blanket to air the bed, put a chicken casserole in the oven and we went to see Paul and Elisabeth. They had been worried about our late arrival. They said that instead of having a New Year meal at St Paradis this year, they had decided to reopen Paul's bistro and have a big party for 40 guests there, with everyone contributing to the food. They asked us to join with them in providing the desserts. Neither of them had been very well and the brunt of the organisation of the event was being borne by Robert and Vincent. We paid our share of the anticipated booze bill.

We mentioned the flies and Elisabeth said they had had the

same problem, as had most other people in the area. Hugo and Hannah had suffered particularly, perhaps because their home, like ours, had been uninhabited for long stretches.

Back in the house, we assembled a new artificial Christmas tree that I had bought as a New Year bargain in Northwich, and fixed its lights. We put it in the kitchen window and left the shutters open, so that its twinkly illuminations would proclaim to the world that the Loaders were in residence again. We also switched on the carriage-lamp by the front door, adding to the street lights which were lit for the first time we could remember.

After supper we started to tackle the flies, vacuuming them up in scores. The live ones were very weak. We started off humanely by spraying them with insecticide to kill them first, but they seemed to be immune to the spray and it had no effect. They buzzed and flapped as drunkenly as before, or lay on their backs waving their legs in the air. Eventually we hardened our hearts and just sucked them into the vacuum cleaner, dead or not. It was only a matter of time before they would expire anyway.

We went to bed with the electric blanket switched to the minimum all-night setting, the 4-tog duvet next to our bodies, and the 12-tog one on top. We woke in the early hours, feeling far too hot, which was a pleasant change after the previous year!

At breakfast time we read the commune bulletin. The mairie was now open between 8am and noon three days a week. There had been five births in the six hamlets which made up the commune. We were delighted to read that Georges and his wife had recently had a baby, Eric. Eric was the only infant in St Paradis. Not counting the few children of families with second homes, the next youngest fulltime inhabitant was probably his own mother! We were pleased because without a new generation the tiny hamlet would wither and die. According to the newsletter, there had been no marriages, five deaths and four burials — presumably of former inhabitants who had died outside the commune. An old lady who lived near Jan and Beatrice had celebrated her 105th birthday.

A page devoted to the archives noted that in 1875 there had been 711 inhabitants including 145 men; 169 houses of which 35 were roofed with tiles or slates and 134 with thatch; 18 horses and mules; 608 "horned" beasts; 2,399 sheep; 72 pigs; 141 carts with two wheels; 160 ovens which could cook 44,800kg of bread in 24 hours (what a strange calculation!); 30 wells and fountains.

In 1880 the church at St Paradis had been enlarged and its attractive bell-tower constructed. The work had been undertaken by a local builder and had cost 5553.88FF. The plans showed two bells and a staircase going up above the gallery where we had seen the bell-ropes hanging through the ceiling. I wondered if the *curé*'s stencilling had dated from this period. The entire church was covered in it, including the plastered walls of the tower. It might have been a device to join the old and new parts of the building in a seamless unity of style.

The commune (current population 230) was busy investing in the future: part of the Mairie building which had once been the mayor's office was being incorporated into a new Salle Polyvalente to replace the old public room and a modern canteen was being created alongside in part of the former school. We promised ourselves that during this visit we really would go to see the new woman mayor and congratulate her on her council's achievements. (As councillors, we knew how rarely anyone ever says "thank you" for your efforts for the community, although brickbats are always in plentiful supply). We had known and liked the former mayor, who had died, but this one was a fount of energy and innovative ideas. She had even introduced a computer into the Mairie and the bulletin had been typed on it.

We went to Stoc with Elisabeth in the morning to buy the things we all needed for the party. After lunch we installed the Godin, temporarily. We put the stove a little way into the room, in front of the fireplace, attached the flexible flue to the back and then pushed this up the chimney as far as it would go. We put blazing logs in its "belly" from the existing fire and waited to see what happened.

The telephone rang. It was Guy and Virginie. They were about to return to Lyon. We dashed round and gave them belated Christmas presents of chocolates (from us) and an Albertine rose (from Roger and Eileen). Guy presented us with a very good bottle of wine. We were sorry that they were going so soon; we had hoped to have a few days overlapping.

Home again, we found that the fire had gone out and re-lit it. In no time the kitchen was a pleasant 18C, which had in the past been hard to achieve with two portable gas fires and a log fire. Throughout the afternoon and evening we experimented with the damper and with a sheet of cardboard which we erected behind the stove to deflect the heat into the room and away from the chimney. Eventually we found the optimum position for the Godin in the room and took down the cardboard. We had expected to miss the roaring log fire, but the red glow from the now-clean door in the stove provided a visual and emotional focal point, too. We were extremely impressed with the little Godin's performance — we were in danger of being warm enough, for once.

Another novel experience was being able to plug electrical gadgets into wall sockets where we needed them, without having to resort to the old orange extension flexes which used to snake all over the floors from the two main sockets in the house. The electrical work which had dominated the previous visit had been well worth while.

Jack installed a new 1000 watt electric convector fire in the study and put the old 500 watt one in the downstairs loo. It raised the temperature enormously even on the lowest setting and we couldn't believe the luxury of being able to do a wee in warmth. Things were becoming alarmingly civilised. Who would believe we had spent the first few days of our occupation sitting in the kitchen on cable drums and a mineral water crate?

Unable to play the CDs we had brought from England, we listened to tapes of Mother's, which we had brought back from her home and hadn't heard before. It was sad to think that she had been able to enjoy them only a few years previously. Now she was much too deaf even to hear them. They took me back to my childhood. Mother had introduced me to classical music by playing records while she did the ironing each week and I sat nearby, curled up in a chair. She had a collection of big heavy 78s, which it was my job to change every few minutes. I forget however many were needed to make up a symphony or concerto. She adored Paul Robeson and the contemporary Russian basses —

and gave me the taste for them too. I felt quite weepy as I listened to her favourites on tape. If I closed my eyes it was as though I was a little girl again, wrapped safely in her love, and she was the one who was looking after me. I wished the roles hadn't needed to be reversed.

Hugo and Hannah came round while they were visiting Paul and Elisabeth. They had successfully moved into the nearby house in October, as planned, and they invited us round there later in the week after the New Year party.

On a frivolous note, I wrote in my diary: "Everyone has noticed my new hairstyle and likes it. They say it makes me look much younger. However old did I look before? Elisabeth, too, has had her hair cut short and we are 'twins'".

On New Year's Eve we did some shopping and looked enviously at the stock of trailers in the local agricultural merchant's yard. After our problem with the deformed tyre in September, Jack had decided that the wheels on ours were too small for the weights we expected it to carry. Unfortunately trailers with bigger wheels were narrower than ours because the wheels had to be mounted outside the body of the trailer and not underneath, as ours were. If we bought a bigger-wheeled trailer we would not be able to cart such wide things about. We decided to stick with what we'd got until it became too decrepit to use.

On the way back we called in at the Mairie to deliver a New Year card to the mayor. She was there, behind the counter in a new extension to the traditional building whose style is familiar over the whole of France: boys' school one side, girls' school the other, and room for weddings and meetings in the middle. She was a bit younger than us, and charming. We thanked her for the improvements we had noted since she had been elected: working street lights (always a boon where the nights are inky-black), big communal wheelie bins shared by groups of houses (instead of the collection of household rubbish sacks put out each Monday in unsightly and unhygienic heaps), well-tended roadsides, and the fascinating commune bulletin.

Back home we arranged the new black sofa and two small chairs in the study and got the computer working so that I could keep my diary on it rather than in a thick red exercise book as before. The padded seat of the typist's chair was rather damp so I tied a polythene bag over it. When my bottom got too cold I stood by the new electric convector heater on the wall, which was conveniently at buttock-height, and warmed myself up. The sofa had also got quite damp en route and we left it to dry out slowly by the heater.

We experimented to see how the Godin would fare on its own without the backup of the open log fire and found that the kitchen reached the same temperature. Sitting beside the woodburning stove was a sensual experience — it was so warm and welcoming. The only snag was that its narrow girth took much shorter pieces of wood than the big fireplace, so Jack had to cut up all the logs with his electric circular saw before we could use them. It became a habit to cut a day's worth at a time.

At 8pm we set off for the party at Paul's old bistro. Jack was wearing his smart French going-out gear of green wool jacket, dark green trousers, bow tie and yellow shirt (which goes down very well in Mornant and, with his beard, makes him look like a French intellectual) and I was in a long paisley shirtwaister from Nightingales, my favourite clothes manufacturer, with beads and matching ear-rings. The dress wasn't very party-ish because I hadn't expected to be invited to something formal. We soon discovered that we were very overdressed. Most male guests were in jeans and very few of the women were wearing skirts. I was the only one in a dress. We must have looked like caricatures of a townie middleclass couple. Most of our neighbours see us covered in dirt and wearing boiler suits or old clothes for the majority of the time, and we hoped that those present who didn't know us wouldn't get the impression we were toffee-nosed and formal.

There were certainly more than 40 guests there. Some had been invited just for drinks and were off to parties of their own later. We heard that a few people, seeing the activity in the building, had thought that the bistro was being reopened and had tried to come in as customers, but Paul didn't have a licence and couldn't serve them. He was very much at home behind the formica-covered bar and was enjoying himself hugely, pressing strong drink on everyone. We declined Ricards and started off with beer. We chatted with Hugo and Hannah and made room for other people in the overcrowded bar by going next door into the former restaurant where the tables for the meal had been set out in a big U-shape. The room was lit by candles in old candelabra and by small night-lights in jam-jars — which provided pools of light and twinkles of atmospheric illumination after the lights were turned out. When the meal started about an hour later, Paul and Elisabeth took pride of place in the hosts' position at the 'top table'. We were on one of the corners with Hugo and Hannah.

We started with oysters and progressed to salmon on toast, mashed tuna, hardboiled eggs with exotic fillings and all sorts of nice things. Each family had contributed a big platter of food and it soon became apparent that there was far too much. They had all added a few extra portions "to be on the safe side" and the big table on which the dishes were displayed before being passed round was groaning with enough delicious titbits to feed a hundred. Chablis and Côtes du Rhône were more or less on tap. We all ploughed on until we couldn't eat another morsel.

The bistro's central heating had been turned on and its big radiators were belting out the heat. Vincent had rigged up a PA system and presumably borrowed records from lots of different people, for the choice of music was 'catholic' to say the least. One moment it was techno and the next, Sasha Distel, Elvis Presley or a traditional accordionist. No one could say their taste was not catered for!

Just before midnight the radio was turned on and everybody counted down the seconds to January 1, 1998. On the dot of midnight, we all cheered, toasted the New Year and went round the room kissing everyone else and wishing them a *Bonne Année* — giving special friends a really big hug for good measure. Then we watched the Dutch go outside to light fireworks and sparklers, joined by the French who sat in their cars with their hands firmly on their hooter buttons. The noise was incredible!

Eating over, everyone concentrated on drinking, chatting and dancing. There were loud cheers when Paul was persuaded to get up and dance. He jiggled about, still wearing his cap, of course, and the women took it in turns to give him a whirl. At nearly 83 he was beaming from ear to ear and in seventh heaven!

Jack and I were so hot that we tended to go in for the slower numbers, but Hannah dragged me out to do "Rockahoola Baby" with her until the sweat ran off me in rivers. She danced with the grace of an 18-year-old. The other women who had turned up in trousers and thick jumpers had by now removed their woollies to reveal pretty evening tops. I usually adopted the layered system of dressing in everyday life, especially at St Paradis, when it could be so cold, but I had stupidly not carried it out tonight. I was stuck, demurely and increasingly stickily, in my long-sleeved ever-so British shirtwaister.

At about 2.15am we decided to go home. We had offered to stay behind to clear up but Hugo said everything was under control and they already had about eight workers lined up. At least two couples were staying the night at the bistro, which used to be a hotel and has a lot of bedrooms. It was built around the turn of the century to serve the busy railway station opposite which is now just a halt on a branch line. At one time it was the place where local farmers brought their produce to send to the markets in Paris, and the commercial travellers stayed there when they made their deals.

Before we left Hugo invited us to a Dutch meal at their new home the following Saturday evening, so we could enjoy one another's company and have a look at the house.

Back at home, we discovered that the Godin had gone out, so Jack relit it to keep the kitchen warm during the night. We went to bed, woke up at about 9am and drifted gently in and out of sleep until about 11am. What a luxury! We hadn't drunk much and had no side-effects from the night before except a certain reluctance to face breakfast.

*It was possible to see clearly where the walls had been raised.*
*Which house could be the one which was swapped for ours?*

# Chapter Thirteen – New Year 1998

At noon we had a brunch of bread and cheese. In the afternoon Jack went out to tend his baby trees and plant some roses which Roger and Eileen had given us. I was sitting in the kitchen reading the Martins' documents when the Vallets arrived to thank us for their Christmas card and invite us for a drink at 6pm. I showed Michel the papers and he said he thought the house which had been swapped was one behind where Paul and Elisabeth lived, which had been sold to the two women who had asked about the wood and prompted us to make contact with the Martins. It seemed to fit the description quite well.

The Martins had also sent us photocopies of photographs they had found amongst Marguerite's effects and had asked us to verify the people they didn't know. Michel instantly recognised Marguerite's father, who had written all the First World War letters we had found. He had been in his thirties or early forties then, but in the picture he was an old man with a thin, tired — almost wistful — face, bright eyes and a long moustache. He was sitting in front of an old polished *armoire* in dark wood, in the kitchen of Marguerite's marital home about 25 miles away. He was wearing a light-coloured working jacket on top of a thick dark shirt, and a wide-brimmed black hat decorated with a ribbon. The photocopy had coarsened the image of what he was holding. It could have been knitting needles or a even barbed wire, but the Martins — who had the original picture — thought he was working with little pieces of wood.

Another photograph showed his bachelor brother, Marguerite's uncle, as an old man. They had lived in our house together. He was in his farming clothes and was pictured outside the front door of a house which looked remarkably like ours, until we studied it in detail and found that the door handles and step did not correspond. He had a flat cap, a working jacket and what appeared to be *sabots*. His hands were large and gnarled and he leaned heavily on a stick. His body was held awkwardly as though he was in pain and I wondered if he had suffered from arthritis. Michel said that he had owned a donkey and cart. The

169

donkey had lived in what we always thought of as our pig-sties. This was the man who, as a teenager in 1877, had covered an expensive textbook with his old homework exercises done in exquisite copperplate writing, wrapped up in a legal parchment from 1746.

Both brothers looked worn out by hard physical work. No wonder they had let the house deteriorate when they were there alone. But they were not ignorant simpletons. We had their books and writings to prove that.

The other photographs were of Marguerite's mother, an unknown woman, and Marguerite's son Alain. One of Alain's pictures was a studio portrait showing him in a white shirt, neat jacket and wide knotted tie, while in the other he was posing outdoors. He had a light coloured mackintosh draped over his shoulders like a cloak, a spotted cravat, an informal jacket and a cigarette between his fingers in a classic 1930s pose of nonchalant elegance. He was probably 18 years old, about to leave his parents' farming community and go to university — full of confidence about what life would bring. My heart went out to him.

The following day we drove over to the *départemental* capital to pay some money into the bank. We went into one of the *bricolages* and found they had a sale of woodburning stoves. There was a wonderful-looking old-fashioned 10kw Godin in black cast iron which we could immediately imagine in the kitchen *cantou*. It was 4790FF, which we could just afford. We had come to realise that life was unimaginable without a Godin — the little second-hand 4kw one had changed our lifestyle completely. A big one would be the answer to our prayers.

We scoured Continent for a *jeté*, unsuccessfully, but bought baby Eric a little present. Then we went on to another *bricolage* to compare Godin prices and found to our frustration that the store was closed for stocktaking.

Back in St Paradis we started to demolish Alex's old kitchen units so that we could remove the tops and replace them with tiled working surfaces, put backs on them to keep out the mice and create a tiled backing panel on the wall to hide the electrical connections and make it all look pretty.

The following day we went to the nearest city on the trail of Godins and *jetés*. It was the time of year when stoves and fires were being sold in abundance. I was nearly seduced into changing my mind and buying a brown woodburning cooker *(cuisinière)* for about 5890FF. Most of our French friends at St Paradis had them (Mornant was not so rural) and I imagined being the owner of the equivalent of an Aga for hundreds of pounds rather than thousands. Visions of me starring in stirring Aga-sagas swam before my eyes. I would love to be Mother Earth, simmering tasty soups on my hob and bringing baby lambs back to life with the incubating qualities of my warm oven. (Though I never did understand how one did that without cooking them or suffocating them). The drawback was that there would have been no visual focus for the kitchen. You can't watch the flames or hot embers in a *cuisinière*. It would have been a shiny big brown box for all the world, and would not have enhanced the 1806 fireplace like a black cast-iron Godin with a glass front and a cheerful orange face.

We could not find a single *jeté* to fit our little black sofa. I knew in my heart of hearts that I was going to have to make one myself when we got back to Cheshire.

Mme Echelle popped in to wish us a happy New Year. We asked after her goats. They had been pregnant last time we had seen them. She said she had decided all her animals were too much trouble. She couldn't go away on visits if she had to worry about the livestock. She had got rid of the goats and geese and a dog had killed the hens and ducks.

"Not the ducks!" we thought.

"You mean the ones on the pond at the end of the little path?" we asked.

"Yes — all gone. We think it was a dog from outside the village, or perhaps a fox."

And that was the last we heard of The Duck with a Dirty Laugh and his friends. The frogs still live on the pond but the water is covered with duckweed and the "WARK, WARK, WARK" of a summer evening is a thing of the past.

We had no trouble finding Hugo and Hannah's new house in the dark. They showed us round and we agreed they had done remarkably well with it in such a short time. They had knocked down a wall downstairs and made most of the ground floor into an right-angular open plan kitchen /dining room/ sitting room, with a *cantou* like ours at one extremity of the "L" and a 13kw Deville woodburning stove in the angle. It heated the whole ground floor to greenhouse temperatures and the heat permeated upstairs into their bedroom. They'd had a parquet floor put in downstairs and installed an ultra-modern Dutch kitchen in grey units, which was stunning. It was too dark to see outside but they shone a torch and we could vaguely see a little building with a bread oven, and a nice garden. It had been raining so hard for days that we didn't venture out to explore in the mud.

Hugo had cooked a traditional Dutch supper of mushroom soup, followed by pork chops, delicious gravy and a mixture of potatoes, carrots and onions bound together with butter. Afterwards we had fruit and coffee. In the course of conversation they told us about their house in Spain, which had a swimming pool. They'd had it built, lived there for about three years and then rented it out when they returned to Holland. When the tenant left they travelled down to Spain to take it over and discovered that the place was filthy and she had stolen the entire contents with the exception of a coffee percolator which didn't work. The police put the case on the file and they got nothing out of the Spanish insurance company — so they lost everything. It didn't bear thinking about.

We got up next morning to discover a horrible burning smell like rubber which we eventually traced to the Godin. We decided it had just got too hot. It had been sold to us as a woodburning stove but we were sure it was really for coke (it said *charbon* on the back). We had been pushing it too far, running it very hot day and night. This made the acquisition of a new big one even more important.

We set to with a vengeance on the kitchen and it soon resembled its normal chaotic state. It had been quite civilised to date!

The following afternoon I took a break from tiling and went to photograph the house which Michel had identified as a candidate for the property swap. The one standing opposite it was a probable, too. On the way past Paul's I bumped into the villager with the drink problem who had helped Jack to build the well cover and who'd so sweetly given me the roses. He was sober and extremely polite. For the first time for years I could carry on a conversation with him. He'd been in hospital for a "cure" a few months previously and everyone had their fingers crossed that it had worked this time. As we chatted, it struck me that, like many of the rural people we knew, he had terrible teeth — especially bad for one so comparatively young. We wondered why this was the case, when the French health service was so excellent. It reminded us of old people of our acquaintance in England who had had all their teeth extracted as a 21st birthday present, the rather illogical argument for such a drastic measure being that they had sparkling new false teeth and (they hoped) no dental expenses in the future.

Next day we were determined to buy the Godin. We compared prices with other places in the *départemental* capital and decided that it was still the best value. Then we had second thoughts, standing in front of it with our chequebook, at 11.30am. For 100FF less we could have a modern brown Deville with a 10kw performance and thermostatic controls. For 500FF more we could have a similar modern Deville with sophisticated controls, decorated with bronze ducks and sheaves of corn(!), which would pump out 13kw like Hugo's furnace. The classic black cast-iron Godin looked beautiful and would harmonise with the ancient *cantou* but it had no thermostatic control. It did, however, have the advantage that it could be fed with fuel from the top, like the little one. We didn't fancy opening the glass fronted doors of the other ones and shoving large logs into the flames. It was the judgment of Solomon. We were so undecided that we agreed to go away, mull it over and come back when the shop reopened at 2pm.

After two hours teetering three ways, we decided on the Godin. We agreed that it would look best in the kitchen and that if one day — in the far distant future — we ever installed central heating, it wouldn't matter if the *poêle* in the kitchen wasn't belting out a macho 13kw. There were no others in stock so we took the Godin which was on display, hoping that nothing was missing. It required three men to carry it out to the estate car and the Peugeot back suspension momentarily sagged under the weight. We wondered how on earth Jack and I would get it out again.

During the 15-mile journey Jack worked out a strategy. He backed the car up to the front door which leads directly into the kitchen. Then he built a little made-to-measure trolley from some oven wheels that Linda's parents had given us and a small piece work top left over from Alex's new kitchen (we provide a good home for everyone's cast-offs). We took off everything that would dismantle − the door, the insides, the lid − and shuffled the carcase out of the boot over a piece of carpet and on to the trolley. We strapped it to the trolley with canoe straps and coaxed it into the kitchen inch by inch. Eventually we had it lined up against the *cantou* wall on its own personal wheels, reassembled and just ready for the next stage in the procedure. We knew there would be no time to fit in during this visit, but we could at least admire it and run our hands over it. We would have had great difficulty buying it during our next visit in late Spring because all the *bricolages* would be busy selling lawn-mowers and garden equipment in the space they devoted to displaying *poëles* in the Winter.

We finally got some salad and *jambon cru* at 5pm, which we thought might be a record for a Loader lunchtime.

Then I settled down to grouting the new tiled work-surfaces and back panel in the kitchen and Jack was equally busy making things. When we had finished, the kitchen units looked wonderful − better than we had ever dared to hope. Before we went to bed we took down the Christmas cards and the Christmas tree, which we left fully decorated for next year and shoved into a polythene bag "fully clothed" for later deposit in the attic. The big kitchen looked very empty and sober without them.

I had promised Hugo and Hannah a proper Balti meal when they came to dinner with us the next evening. Unfortunately I couldn't buy any fresh ginger or spinach locally, so I had to make do with variations on a variety of green lime curry in a jar which was rather insipid because I made it go too far. I suppose they couldn't tell the difference but I could, and as the star Balti cook of Hartford, I was disappointed. Chris and Linda had introduced us to this method of cooking when they were living in Stoke and working for Michelin in their 'work experience' year, long before we had bought the Peugeot. Baltis had just spread from Birmingham's Asian community but restaurants serving them were few and far between. The pair had raved about a little Balti restaurant they had found, where you ordered your food then waited for it over a pint at the pub next door because the restaurant didn't have a licence. When it was ready the waiters would come and get you. They gave you enormous portions and aluminium containers to take home the excess to eat for lunch the next day.

Chris and Linda rang up one morning and said: "Would you like to come out for a special Balti supper with us tonight?"

We had said: "What a lovely idea, of course we would."

Then they added: "Could you bring the Carlton estate because we want to move some furniture afterwards..."

We had to hand it to them!

Our time in St Paradis was coming rapidly to a close, though this was our longest New Year visit. Jack put a bolt and hinges on the door which led from the front of the bread oven building into the hayloft above it, which had fallen in earlier in the winter. It was usually just held by being wedged against the door-frame, but we wanted something more secure. Once more I was ashamed of my frailty. Not only do I get lost in half-acre woods, but I am scared of heights and I loathe ladders. However much I rationalise it, I simply can't climb up a ladder more than about five feet off the ground. One of the bravest things I've ever done was to climb out of a lock connecting the Worcester Canal and the River Severn when we were in a narrowboat. It was high (by my standards), perhaps about ten feet, with a sheer drop into the river. I was utterly petrified. I only did it because otherwise I would still be there on the bottom rung. It didn't seem sensible to spend the rest of my life in a lock. I often wonder what I would do if I was on a sinking Channel ferry and was expected to climb down into a lifeboat.

Helping Jack with the bread oven hayloft door required climbing six or seven feet up a ladder. I might just have done that but the stone flowerbed was in the way and instead of being at a normal angle the ladder was sloping at about 60 degrees to miss the edge of the rocks. This meant that I could see the ground between the rungs. I suppose "don't look down" should be the motto but you've got to look at the rungs to see where they are and if there is a flowerbed yawning away four feet below it's terrifying. I would go three feet up the ladder, stand on tip-toe and hand things to Jack at the fullest extension of both our arms. Writing this, I can't believe I could be so stupid, but at the time I had a complete mental block about going any higher. The problem is that my brain tells me if I go one centimetre above what I consider to be safe then I will definitely, inevitably fall off and break lots of bones very painfully. Indeed, if I don't fall off naturally, then I will be forced simply to throw myself off. It is quite an extraordinary feeling.

In my defence I suppose I should add that I'm not a complete wimp. I enjoy driving cars, riding horses and sailing dinghies. I'm not scared of most four-legged animals though I'm not keen on anything with more than four legs. I think mice are sweet and I've disposed of quite a few dead rats. But I don't like ladders. Or fire. Or putting my head under the bedclothes. But that's another story.

I suppose I'm not wildly enthusiastic about chain-saws, either, but Jack was determined to try out the one he had bought in the autumn. He got togged up in face mask, gloves, steel toe-capped boots and forest-workers' trousers. I armed myself with thick gloves and some goggles. We took the car and trailer down to the Martins' wood and, singing Monty Python's "Lumberjack Song", we chopped up all the dead trees which we could find on the ground. Mme Echelle's son came over on his moped out of curiosity, to see what was happening in a wood which had been untended for much of his lifetime. He noted all Jack's protective gear and they chatted about chain-saws. He mentioned in passing that his father had nearly cut his leg off with one when he went to get a hanky out of his trouser pocket. Jack made a policy decision to let his own nose run in future.

We loaded the wood into the trailer and drove home with it proudly. It had been great fun. We stacked the small logs neatly in the barn and started to cut up the larger pieces of tree which had been too cumbersome to do on the spot. One piece had foliage still attached and as I moved it round I didn't notice that some of the twigs were dislodging a 7ft plank of wood stored against the side of the barn. It fell on the side of my head, just missing my eye, knocked me silly for a few moments and gave me a nice big bruise on the temple. It was ironic that just picking up a branch had turned out to be more dangerous in real life than climbing up a perfectly safe ladder.

The weather was like Spring on our last full day at St Paradis. We revelled in it and so did the wretched flies until they got the vacuum cleaner treatment. They just seemed to queue up to die on the windowsills. I would hoover up thirty terminal casualties, unplug the cleaner to go to the next window, turn back and find another thirty gathering in their place ready to drop down dead or thrash around on their backs.

I thought I would take advantage of the sunshine to photograph the buildings in the village which might possibly qualify as being involved in the property swap. The more I looked at Michel's choice, the more doubtful I was.

The long and complicated legal document, signed on April 8, 1883, said the properties belonging Monsieur and Madame Barberon, the more distant members of the family, who were described as *propriétaires cultivateurs*, were (fairly briefly!):

1. A straw-thatched building comprising a house having two rooms on the ground floor, two rooms on the first floor, an attic over all, a double stable for cows with a granary over, a barn and a single *stable for cows with a hayloft, all of them under the same roof, plus two small thatched stables for hens and pigs built as a lean-to on the north east gable of the house, all joining the meadow and the public road (**our house before it was given a slate roof**).

2. A field of 95 *ares* (an *are* is 100 sq metres), joining the afore-mentioned building, two other fields, the lane which goes beside

the church and the road to the next village (**our field**).

3. A garden of name unknown of 3 *ares* (**down the little lane to the side of our house, retained by the Martins**).

4. A piece of land called *Le Petit Bois* of 6 *ares* in area (**maybe 'our' wood?**).

In return, Marguerite's grandparents and widowed great-grandfather, who was unable to sign his own name, described only as *cultivateurs* (who by definition rented their farm land and were thus socially inferior to the Barberons but presumably went up the social scale by dint of the transaction), exchanged:

1. A thatched house comprising one room on the ground floor, one bedroom on the first floor, with an attic over all, and a small lean-to bedroom constructed behind the house with a little room serving as a *cave* and dairy, covered with tiles, all of these adjoining a **cowshed (the two property descriptions vary between *une ecurie a vaches* and **une étable* — I don't know if it is significant) and the public road.

2. A cowshed joining the above house, the house belonging to X and the public road.

3. A garden of 2 *ares* (joining several others whose owners are named).

4. A barn known as the New Barn with a grain store at the side, covered with tiles and joining the public road, the stable of Y and the hempfield mentioned below.

5. A hempfield called The Hempfield of 6 *ares* joining the barn, the yard of Z, and numerous other properties.

At first glance Michel's choice seemed obvious. It was a small house with a lean-to out the back and an adjoining cowshed. It was built straight on to a little public road. But the cowshed did not adjoin any other house. It did have a small garden but on the current map of the village this was bigger than 2 *ares* and only joined a couple of others, rather than those described in the document. There was a barn with a tiled roof and an open "first floor" part, not far from us, which corresponded with the description of the New Barn, but its situation was not as described. It might have had a 6 *ares* hempfield beside it, but this was on an island of land between roads and a public footpath and certainly didn't correspond with the description.

Every time I pored over the map and exclaimed "Eureka!" I had to admit later that I was wrong. The individual bits of the jigsaw were identifiable, but they did not piece together. It was intensely frustrating. I decided that the only answer was to photograph absolutely everything and peruse it all at leisure afterwards.

One fascinating point was that I had read that in the late 1800s, when people became affluent enough to replace their steeply sloping thatch roofs with slate (or cheaper *tuiles*) which needed a less steep angle, they raised the walls to make the upper storeys higher. Once you were aware of this, you could see the evidence everywhere. In nearly all the houses in the village with slate roofs I could trace clearly new stone in the gable ends and front and back walls, showing where the height had been raised. It was possible to see instantly which buildings had once had thatched roofs, and which were built after slate or *tuiles* were standard roof coverings. Looking at our own house, this was obvious too — except at the front where the owners had invested in a posh new facade where the beautiful pointing obliterated all traces of an extension upwards. At the back, it was plain to see, and corresponded with the height of the barn, which had been tiled but not altered. The owners did not need a higher barn roof. We could see that it had once fitted the 1883 description of a house and barn all under the same thatched roof. Inside, it was possible to see differences in the plastering of the wall at to the stairs and landing and to guess that the tiny window on the landing which allowed the house to breathe through its gauze covering had once been there to ventilate an attic. Once the roof was raised, windows of classical proportions could be pierced in the fabric of the building.

Once again, the latent historian in me longed to know exactly what had happened to the house. Had Marguerite's grandparents, the new owners, done so well that they had immediately set about "doing up" their new acquisition according to the latest architectural fashions? The 1870s and '80s were a time of prosperity for farmers in the Limousin — perhaps the only time of prosperity, for life had been hard before and was certainly hard again during and after the First World War. Marguerite's great-grandfather had been unable to write his own name, yet her uncle and father had benefited from the Education Acts of the 1870s and had written beautifully. They were well educated and bright: perhaps, like Alain, they would have gone on to different careers if a life in agriculture had not been expected of them. In the attic we had some of the books and catalogues which they had received regularly. They had been very modern farmers for their day, putting into practice all the latest theories. Marguerite had been well educated too. She loved writing letters and, the Martins told us, had longed to be a writer. I hoped she was pleased that I pursued my own writing craft in a study converted from her old bedroom and that I was writing about her — even though, to protect her privacy, it was under one of her Christian names that she hadn't used. The spirited person who had occasionally spoken to me through telepathy would probably have relished the chance to have a go on my computer. A photo of her aged 20, full of hope and happiness, hung in my office at home, as an inspiration and a companion. I often chatted to her when I was stuck.

Also intriguing was the question of why the Barberons had decided to swap their nice big house and land for an assortment of bits and pieces and a smaller house. Was it a clue or a red herring that the old *auberge* where Mme Echelle now lived still bore their family name in faded painted letters? Had they decided to stop farming and start an *auberge*? Or was that run by entirely different people called Barberon? The *auberge* had certainly been the centre of village life in the old days, and if St Paradis was growing and prosperous in the 1880s it would have been a good business.

After I had done my photographs of the village (ending up with an A4 page full of theories about the house swap!) and run out of film, Jack and I decided to go up the hill and deliver Eric's present. There was no one at Georges' house so we went over to the cemetery opposite to say "hello" to Marguerite. It was still a gorgeous day and we lingered, for the first time going round all the graves. Several marked deaths in the First World War, or through accidents. Many were memorials to babies and children. Let no one ever say, as I have read, that before birth control people were philosophical about the inevitable deaths of their children. They weren't. The hurt and anguish in the gravestone inscriptions cry out across the generations. Mothers risked death to bear each child and each one, I am sure, was treasured even if its birth might have been inconvenient. The French, in any case, were quite well informed about contraception, and the complicated inheritance laws which decreed the break-up of property were an incentive to keep down the size of their families.

That evening, Paul and Elisabeth came around for their ritual "end of holiday" supper with us. It's impossible to repay their kindness and constant hospitality but we always try to spend the last night with them each time we are in St Paradis. It's a shame that we can't give them a really slap-up dinner but they are used to having their main meal in the middle of the day and don't have room for a lot more food in the evening. We are rarely well enough organised to prepare a big meal at lunchtime — and would go to sleep all afternoon if we ate one!

Almost the last task before the journey home on Saturday, January 10 was to estimate the height of the house so that we could order some stainless steel flue liner for the new Godin. We measured the height of the kitchen, our bedroom and the attic to its highest point, then added a bit to account for the chimney. It came to nine and a half metres.

It was so warm outside that we were able to wander round in sweaters rather than anoraks and gloves, as we would have expected in January. It seemed as if Nature was grossly over-compensating for the appalling winter the year before.

If Nature was helping outside, then Fate was helping inside. The little Godin had single-handedly brought the kitchen temperature up to 22C each day, which we had rarely achieved with the log fire and portable gas heaters. It was a pleasant kind of warmth, too — we didn't like the atmosphere created by the gas fires. It was such a novel experience to be at St Paradis and to be warm enough, that we almost couldn't believe it. The £50 we had invested in the little *poële* was the best money we'd ever spent.

"Thank God for the Godin," we said, fervently, as we drove away.

*There were lots of children's ponies for sale at the horse fair*

# Chapter Fourteen – May 1998

The lead-up to our visit to St Paradis in May 1998 was hectic. I was busy publishing a novel by a local author and needed to get it to the binders before we went on holiday, so that I could start to market it when we returned and launch it at the beginning of July. At the last minute I was asked to do some freelance writing too, which was very interesting but threw out my carefully calculated timescale. They say work expands to fill the time available and it's true. I gave the freelancing priority and crammed the rest of the tasks into the small hours.

We had had some worrying moments with Mother, who was now only a few months short of ninety. The paranoia seemed to return in more frequent cycles, in spite of the medicine which had previously kept it at bay. She thought people at the hospital day unit were plotting against me because they resented the new camel coat and squashy velvet hat I'd bought in the sales after we had returned from France. She was certain they didn't like me, because I had written a book. She was in despair about what to wear for the small family dinner with the children to celebrate my 50th birthday in January and talked about nothing else for a fortnight until I could have gone down the garden and screamed. She goaded me about trivial things until I wept with frustration — then, of course, she was mortified and I was furious with myself for losing control in front of her. I was constantly at the point where if anyone had said "boo!" to me I would have broken down. In the previous 50 years we'd quite literally never had a cross word. She had been a perfect mother, I loved her unconditionally and we had always been soulmates. The change in her character was almost too cruel to bear. Her drugs were altered at one point and she had a violent reaction to them, hardly being able to walk without a stick or speak without slurring her words. The new medicine was stopped and allowed to clear out of her bloodstream before another sort was prescribed. This worked reasonably well, and with no physical side effects, thank goodness. Mother's dreams when she dozed off became more vivid and got to the point when she did not know if she was awake or asleep.

One day she told me she had had a terrible night because she did not know if she was dead or alive. Not long afterwards I went to fetch her from the hospital day unit and she said she was dying. She was so certain that I took her word for it. We said a moving goodbye in the car. She wasn't at all upset. She had been widowed for 20 years and was looking forward to rejoining my father and seeing her parents again. Auntie and I packed her off to bed and we took turns to sit up with her all night. She slept from 6pm until about 7am — which was unheard-of — then woke up and talked in a confused manner about being in an air crash. After a few hours she became bored in bed, couldn't understand what the fuss was about, and got up. I had prepared myself mentally for her to die peacefully in her sleep and adjusting to the fact that she hadn't done caused a wave of conflicting emotions. The hospital warned me that things could only get worse and I steeled myself for the crisis I felt sure would loom in the summer. I was racked with guilt at the thought that I couldn't cope much longer.

Against this background we were desperate for a break at St Paradis. We hoped to have visits from Georges and Chantal, the Martins and a Hartford couple with a house in Deux-Sèvres.

We packed the trailer on May Bank Holiday Monday and put the cover on temporarily. The main item of furniture was a china cabinet which had been given to us by our neighbours. We decided we would put it on the landing at the French house and use it to display some of the "treasures" we had found there. The weather was awful and we managed to pop the last things in the trailer on the Thursday morning before we set off — it had been too wet to take the tarpaulin off before then.

At a frenetic pace we finally managed to get everything done and to leave earlier than usual because the ferry departure time had been brought forward. The early start paid off and we were never stationary on the M6. At Portsmouth we joined the queue on the dockside and ate a leisurely supper in the car. We saw a large new catamaran at the quayside which was due in commission shortly. Work on it was being finished off. The tide was so high and the companionway up to the 'cat' was at such a steep angle that the people climbing up it were going on all fours and those coming down were descending backwards, as if it were a ladder. The exception was one man carrying heavy things on his shoulder who was racing up two steps at a time!

Looking for our cabins we were perplexed because they had just changed the naming convention of the decks. Instead of being A-J they were numbered and it was quite hard to find our cabin because the serial numbers on the ticket had been printed badly and we couldn't read them — and neither could anyone else.

Jack slept very well because he was so tired after driving 250 miles and coping with his extra workload in the run-up to the trip. My sleep was fitful and I was made wide awake by a woman of questionable parentage calling in a loud braying voice to her daughter just after I had finally dropped off. It must have been 1am (English time). Cabin doors banged for what seemed like most of the night. Maybe people don't realise that the private little boxes which make up modern ferry cabins have very thin walls and are not soundproof. The other passengers are out of sight and out of mind — but they are still trying to get to sleep.

We disembarked just after 7am French time and stopped to eat some sandwiches at our usual place. We were about to go and get some coffee when a coach party appeared and we gave up, knowing there was no hope of being served for ages.

In contrast with the English weather, it was gorgeous. In fact it was too hot in the afternoon after we got back in the car following our ritual shopping stop at Orléans. It was 35°C inside and in the high 20°Cs outside and we were glad we had a cool box in which to put the perishable food. Naturally, I had packed all the wrong clothes to deal with a heatwave.

After a time we began to wonder if it was an official public holiday in France. It was certainly the anniversary of the liberation in 1945. There were *tricolours* everywhere and sometimes we saw official-looking gatherings at the *mairies* as we passed. Many businesses and factories seemed to be closed. It was hard to get out of the English habit of expecting most public holidays to be observed at the weekend or on a Monday. After all, we had just had May Day. Our thoughts turned to Alain, who had died two days before VE-Day, 43 years ago. We usually remembered him on May 4 and we were ashamed that we had not done this year.

We arrived at St Paradis at 4.30pm. When we unpacked the trailer we went into the barn and discovered that our firewood for the next year had been delivered and left in a large pile in the central section. Jack spotted that several tiles had come off the barn roof at its highest point — much too high for him to deal with. We hadn't got a ladder long enough and he didn't have a head for those sort of heights anyway. It was well over 30 feet.

In the study I put my home-made *jeté* on the little sofa. I had given up hope of finding one and had bought vast quantities of heavy cream material at IKEA, joined it up in the right shape and trimmed it with fabric to match the cushions in the room. The result was actually much more attractive than a measly bought *jeté* and I regretted the wasted hours ferreting round supermarkets looking for a ready-made one.

At about 6.30pm we went over to Paul and Elisabeth, who were sitting with Hugo and Hannah on the terrace having a drink. They said the weather had been terrible here too, and that it had changed today in our honour! Storms this week had been responsible for the tiles coming off the barn but it had not rained since, or Paul would have got someone to replace them. He suggested that Mme Echelle's son would be happy to do it.

"He goes up and down ladders like a rabbit," said Paul. We loved the simile: we didn't know French rabbits could climb ladders.

A little later Michel joined us from the neighbouring kitchen garden where he had been working. He was too shy to stay long but shortly afterwards his wife came to have a chat and ask the others if they wanted her to get any cheeses from the merchant who was due in the village the next day. The travelling shops are vital to villages like St Paradis and they reflect the lifestyle of the inhabitants: on various days of the week you can buy bread and cakes, meat and *charcuterie*, basic groceries, and a big selection of cheese and sausages. If you had to live on these provisions, the menu would be repetitive and quite dear, but acceptable. You would be expected to grow your own vegetables, of course. Every few months, big lorries packed with tools or catalogue-type clothes come and park in the town square. Their presence is advertised on colourful circulars brought by the postman.

We enquired after Paul's health. He said his eyes were now OK but his heart wasn't too good any more. He apologised for not doing much in our garden because it had been far too muddy. We thanked him for what he had done — especially at the front where the ground was solid. He had weeded round the proper plants at the back although he sensibly hadn't attempted to clear the nettles, thistles and grass which had grown back over the area which will one day be a terrace. Those weeds must be the most tenacious in the world! They are constantly being cut down and poisoned but they always come back for more.

Our friends reminded us that it was the weekend of the big May horse fair. We had been in 1996 but we had simply forgotten to go last year. We had been thinking about the twinning and the Martins' forthcoming visit and it had slipped our minds.

We returned home and had salad and beefburgers for supper. Then Jack tried to connect the computer up to the Internet. I had opened an Internet account the previous month, to advertise my little business and to enable us to use e-mail. We had also joined a global roaming scheme so that we could use e-mail in France to communicate with our next door neighbours who were looking after book orders for me, to write to Chris and Linda, and to be available generally if people wanted to get in touch.

Hugo had warned us a few hours before that it was very complicated in France (where anything which conceivably can be complicated always is!). In England you just plug the modem into the phone socket and it works, but not over here. We had bought the gubbins we wanted in Orléans but it wasn't playing. (We discovered later that it was faulty). Frustrated that his usual genius with things electronic was not being effective, Jack gave up and we went to bed. He was not able to get the connection working for several days.

We got up early and were enchanted to see three big hunting dogs — presumably belonging to one of Mme Echelle's sons — go hurtling down the road just bursting with *joie de vivre*, tails and ears trailing in the breeze. A few minutes later their owner came past in a little car, towing a small trailer with a grille at the back. Through this grille were staring the grinning faces of three more hunting dogs. He drove round the back of Michel's kennels to a chorus of barking and then emerged where the road came out again to meet ours, at top speed, with about seven smiling doggy faces looking out of the back grille as the animals jostled for position. They were in paroxysms of excitement over what was in store. It was hilarious. Wherever the trailer went it took with it a chorus of woofs. We decided it must be the hunting season.

We drove to the capital of the *département* to pay our travellers' cheques into the bank. It was busy and there was only one cashier on. After a time the manager himself saw the queue building up and, very democratically, he came down out of his ivory tower to help out behind the counter. One dapper elderly man wanted to cash a cheque quickly and we just knew that he was going to jump into our place, although we had been waiting much longer than he had. It amused us that as soon as the manager arrived on the scene the chap left the queue behind us and thrust his cheque into the boss's hands with hardly a word of explanation, as though he had a special right to preferential treatment. There was none of the usual polite conversation. We wondered if he had lots of money on deposit and was a customer to be appeased at all costs.

Then we went on to the town where we had bought our house from the local *notaire*. We were nostalgic about being there: our previous memories were of being all worked up inside that everything would go wrong with the transaction. It has an attractive fountain in the centre and is famous for its ancient castle where a Turk was imprisoned in Crusader times. Georges (from Mornant) had recommended a local stockist of stainless steel flue and we had ordered what we wanted by fax from Cheshire the previous month. The proprietor was very nice and spoke English extremely well. I complimented him on it and he said I had written the original fax in very good French. We basked in one another's approval. We arranged to return with the trailer on Tuesday afternoon to collect it all.

Back in the capital, we bought food for the next few days and treated ourselves to eight baby geranium plants to put on the kitchen windowsill. We both hate the smell of geraniums but we hoped they might deter the flies and add ethnic authenticity to the house. We knew we could find them cheaper at the horse fair, but they would be difficult to carry round.

After lunch at 3pm Jack went out with the brush cutter and chopped down all the weeds at the back and front. It's always one of his first tasks when we arrive — he wants to stamp his authority on the vegetation. I helped him occasionally after I'd done the unpacking and various household chores, getting stung on the feet by cut nettles as I walked over them in ordinary shoes. Then I put on my wellingtons and we "beat the bounds" of the estate. In spite of the recent bad weather the field was not too wet. Georges the agricultural contractor had cut some more drainage channels, and perhaps these had helped. The field had not been grazed so it was full of hay, flowers and thistles, which we thought should make a tasty meal for the cows when it was mown. We hoped Georges could cut it this year without getting his tractor bogged down.

While we were out the back, I could swear I heard a corncrake. I'm no ornithologist but I had listened to a radio programme about the bird not long before and the call was very distinctive. I was pleased because I knew they were rare.

We had supper on the table outside, underneath our parasol, with a special citronella candle burning to keep flies and flying insects away. We had left the meal almost too late, at 9.15pm, as it was getting dark and turning cold. From this vantage point we spotted the hunting dogs coming back from an exciting day out.

As Jack was locking up before we went to bed, he was surprised to find a large toad sitting under the stairs by the back door, staring at him. We left it to its own devices, firmly shutting the door which connects the under-stairs area with the kitchen.

We got up early to go to the fair. Two years earlier we had arrived there about 11am but had felt it was a bit too late and that we had missed out. This time we were there by 9.30am. As we parked outside the town cemetery we saw Jan and Beatrice. Elisabeth had told us that they had stopped renting their apartment in Amsterdam and come to live permanently in France. We walked the half-mile into town with them and they invited us for supper that night. Beatrice complimented me on my short auburn hair and said it made me look younger. (I was beginning to get a complex about the "younger" bit!). I replied that you have to start thinking about these things when you're fifty. Beatrice is sixty-seven but she looks in her fifties...

As we walked up the hill we saw a little boy proudly leading a baby donkey, with his father bringing up the rear. They had obviously just bought it. The donkey wasn't very happy and stopped. Perhaps it was missing its mother. The boy went ahead the length of the leading rein and pulled. The father smacked the little animal on the rear. Anyone who knows how to lead a horse could have told them that sort of handling was totally counter-productive. The donkey wouldn't go forwards. The last we saw of them, as we went round a bend, the donkey was at right angles across the road refusing to budge and holding up the traffic.

We split up from Jan and Beatrice at the crossroads and walked down to look at the poultry traders. Then we set off for the horse market, which we had only visited perfunctorily two years before in the misty drizzle. You could trace your way there by following the sound of the whinnies. In today's gorgeous weather there were far more animals for sale and the atmosphere of the whole event was quite different. Hundreds of animals of all descriptions in headcollars or halters were tied up to the railings. Others were loose in pens with a dealer's name written on a board and tied to the front. Many were being led around by sellers or new owners.

We saw a dark gypsy boy riding a beautiful grey pony bare-back with only a halter, wheeling round dramatically and show-ing off its paces. His companion — perhaps his father — had curled white moustaches and spoke in *patois*, which sounds like a mixture of French and Latin.

I was struck by how docile most of the horses were. One small brown pony was very cross about being tied up and left alone. It had pawed quite a large a hole in the ground, tossing its head and mane and whinnying in annoyance. It was the exception. I had always been brought up to beware of a horse's heels but in the tight squeeze of the horse fair there was no option — they were tied so that the public "corridor" was between scores of backsides. These backsides were loaded with not only the potential to lash out with hard hooves, but also to pee or crap all over passers-by. However, I didn't see a single horse try to kick anyone. Dark yellow urine ran everywhere in steaming rivulets, and there was little point in trying to miss treading in the dung. As Joyce, who left us the money to buy the house, would have said: "It's only digested grass." She used to muck out the horsebox with her bare hands and was scornful of the more squeamish among the riders at her stables.

The animals ranged from heart-tugging Shetland pony foals to worn-out Percheron farm horses, white with age and dozing on their feet. There were scores of children's ponies and some nice quality hacks. To judge by the number of trotting carts and pony traps around, perhaps many of the animals had been trained for pulling vehicles rather than being ridden.

There were lots of donkeys and mules. We'd been told that donkeys were now fashionable pets in a country where most families were rooted in the soil and could dredge up a relative somewhere with some grazing. I hoped the people who had bought them knew how to look after them. The mules were another matter. I could imagine them being popular in a peasant culture but not, surely, in France. Donkeys were pretty but mules were workers. I had never seen them being used on farms, certainly not in this area, where 1950s tractors were still commonplace.

We wandered among the rows of animals, me with more than a few misgivings. I don't like livestock markets much because I always identify with the animals rather than their human handlers. I was critical but what I noticed here would also be normal and unremarked upon in any country market in England. I was pleased there was a big sign over the horse fair warning that cruelty to animals was an offence and would not be tolerated. Gendarmes circulated freely and would presumably have stopped any ill-treatment. But I didn't like to watch dealers idly poking their bored ponies with sticks to make them look more interesting, or the cuts on the backs of a foal's hind legs where it had perhaps resisted being loaded into a horsebox. Most of the animals were in good condition but some were very thin with pronounced pelvises and sparse coats. Would they be nursed back to health or left, thin and ill, to their own devices? Some owners had groomed their ponies but others were dirty and had been brought straight from the field covered in mud. Several foals were very young and I hoped they were being sold with their mothers.

I stopped to talk to a mule. I had never met one face-to-face before. He seemed delighted and surprised to be given some affection. He was tethered in a simple rope halter but had sore patches on his wide forehead where an ill-fitting headcollar had chafed for days or months on end. I desperately wanted to take him home, get him a tailor-made bridle and give him some love. We had a big field and special donkey-sized stables as well as cow-stalls in the barn. But whatever would I do with a mule? His sad trusting face stayed on my conscience for months.

I stroked the vast head of a barrel-chested Percheron, standing patiently with her eyes half-closed under white lashes. She had so much weight and power — and yet was so gentle. She snuffled in response and leaned gently towards me. I was taken back to my childhood. When I was little, we had a cart-horse in the field at the bottom of our garden and they were still used on the farms. By the time I was a pony-mad teenager the local Shires and Percherons on my friends' farms were being pensioned off as workers, but they were still being bred for showing in specialist studs nearby. The flower nursery where Joyce had her riding school still had a crew-yard and stables with massive Suffolk Punches on the pay-roll. As Michel always said, horses didn't compact the land with their weight like a tractor.

When I got near the horses to pat them, their distinctive equine smell was intoxicating. I wanted to forget that I was an eleven-stone fifty-year-old and jump on their patient backs, put my arms round their necks and bury my face in their manes, like I had as a child. These rough and ready animals, at the bottom end of the horsy market, reminded me of Joyce's hardy ponies and horses, who spent most of their lives grazing on the river bank. I had met Jack through Joyce. She was his mother's cousin and had given him the chance of an outdoor life as a boy. He helped her to build and maintain her stables and, eventually, after a pony-trekking holiday with the Scouts, had decided to learn to ride, too. We had met when I was 14 and he was 18. I had taught him to ride a horse down the local country lanes, pedalling alongside on my bicycle, shouting instructions until it was time for me to have a go. He had taught me his sport, dinghy sailing. We had been together ever since. Joyce had shaped our lives. She had brought us together and then left us the money to buy the house. We were totally indebted to her.

I fantasised. When we retired to France we would buy a middle-aged mare, and perhaps a tired mule "in need of a good home" to keep her company. The horse would be big and kind and not interested in bucking me off or running away with me. At my age, I didn't think I would bounce if I was thrown — I had unpleasant memories of falling off on to my head, aged about 12, being concussed and having an out-of-the-body experience which probably meant I nearly went to meet my Maker. The mare and I would wander the lanes round St Paradis together at a leisurely pace. The exercise would keep me fit and I would be known as the eccentric Englishwoman with the horse. If Jack was interested, we would perhaps forgo the mule and have two horses, so that we could go riding together — which would be wonderful. We would pay Michel or Georges to look after the animals when we went back to visit England...

I tore myself away, past the pen of Percheron foals, bigger than some of the ponies but still with curly baby tails and dark coats which would lighten with age. We went down to the commercial stands. They weren't like the smart ones you find at English county agricultural shows. Indeed very few of the people present were like the English horsy set. Presumably the French horsy set also bought and sold their animals through advertisements in the trade press and by word of mouth, rather than at a traditional fair. The folk here were farmers, dealers and country people who, by and large, regarded horses as part of the scenery, possible ingredients for lunch and a commodity to be traded. When I heard two men talking about the assets of a *blond*, I assumed they were referring to a horse or a cow.

The stalls reflected this pragmatism. The tack was cheap and probably wouldn't have been particularly comfortable for the rider or the horse. The bargain headcollars were stiff and unlikely to soften up with regular applications of saddle-soap. I had noticed that the mules and donkeys seemed to come off worst where tack was concerned. Their headcollars were as stiff as boards with dried mud, and looked as though they had never been cleaned. This must have caused a lot of unnecessary discomfort. I could see the sense now in the weekly tack-cleaning I'd done as a girl, to keep the leather soft and supple.

A young woman at the largest stand wanted to buy a whip. It wasn't a riding whip — as carried elegantly by MFHs — but more of a bull-whip, made from plaited brown leather. She lashed it in the air, trying to crack it and nearly catching herself on the end of the nose. "It's too short!" she cried. But she bought it and walked off hand-in-hand with her man. What did she want it for? Were they into sado-masochism, or lion-taming?

Jack and I wended our way into the crowds flanking the horse pens. All this was the serious part of the fair, where the dealers and customers would spend most of their day, so naturally there was a bar serving wine, manned by a dark-haired glamorous barmaid with bright red lips, looking bored as she wiped up the slops on the counter.

As we walked back towards the town centre, the crowds were multiplying — the warm sunshine had obviously drawn them in from far and wide. We decided there were two distinct sorts of clientele — the country people who arrive early, go to see the horses and buy useful things at the fair which they couldn't find otherwise, and the town people out for a day trip, to do some impulse shopping and to enjoy the festive atmosphere. As we *paysans* were going home, the others were arriving and there was a nasty impasse at one narrow part of the street where it was almost impossible to go forwards or back. Cardboard boxes full of ducklings were held at head-height above the crush, together with pots of geraniums, and families battled to keep together. It was momentarily unpleasant and we were glad to get out of it.

The market traders were doing more business than they had two years before, the fine weather having put customers in the mood to spend. This part of the fair echoed to the sounds of traditional accordion music coming from the stands selling tape cassettes and CDs, and I was tempted to buy until I reasoned that I would never purchase such things from a market stall in England in case they turned out to be bootleg and terrible quality. *Caveat emptor!* I did buy some asparagus, from one of the many competing stalls selling it.

At home we stacked the firewood neatly in the barn then Jack cleared the double cowshed and rigged up a portable fluorescent light so that he could use his circular saw in there and not spread sawdust all over the salon. I put the "treasures" on display in the china cabinet on the landing. It was an ideal place for them: people could see them but there was no direct light to fade or damage them.

At 6.30pm we drove round to Jan and Beatrice, taking some wine for them and some dog biscuits wrapped in ribbon as a joke present for their two beautiful dogs, Gamine — now 13 — and her daughter Crissette. The couple were currently deeply enmeshed in the famous net of French bureaucracy, while they tried to get a residence permit, register their car and obtain all the documentation which is required when you move from one country to another. We didn't fancy wading through the same procedure, one day.

First thing the following morning, Jack made a box to hold the geraniums on the windowsill and one of our neighbours came past with a tractor and muck-spreader for the first of many, many trips throughout the day to take manure down the little track to the right of the house into one of the fields which is otherwise inaccessible. The countryside is criss-crossed with these narrow overgrown paths which lead off the roads and only impinge on the consciousness when their presence is indicated by wide tractor tyre-tracks cutting swathes through the grass and brambles.

Paul brought across a letter (the postman delivers our mail to him even when we are in St Paradis!). It was from the Martins, saying that couldn't come to see us because they'd had to return to Paris unexpectedly. We were sorry because although we exchanged letters regularly, it was great to be with them in person.

We pottered about. I ventured in to the back of the bread-oven building and found a spectacular pile of owl droppings about a foot high and 18 inches across, underneath where an old cat-ladder hung on the wall. From the feathers stuck to the rungs, it was obvious that the well-fed bird used it as a perch.

The weather was glorious and at noon I decided to be truly decadent and have a glass of wine while sitting outside in the sun at the back of the house. When I shut my eyes the sounds were marvellous. If someone had taped them, I would have known immediately that the recording was of St Paradis. I could hear all sorts of birds, both wild and domestic: woodpigeons, song thrushes, the corncrake, a cockerel and many others which I couldn't identify. Against the background of these, bored gun-dogs were baying from their kennels and some cows which had been moved to a new meadow were mooing to their former companions across the hedge. Then in the distance someone was cutting grass and weeds with a big motorised strimmer and the farmer's muck-spreader was trundling up and down a nearby field. Under the trees was the lazy hum of insects, maybe honey bees, wasps and hornets, which might — or might not — be a threat. When I opened my eyes, swifts or swallows were darting about in the sky.

I could have stayed in the sunshine with my wine forever, but I went inside to make the lunch. I was looking forward to eating the asparagus we'd bought the day before. We've been served heavenly *asperges* in France and it is my favourite vegetable. I peeled the stems of some of the bunch and decided they were so tough that only a pressure cooker would make an impression. It was difficult to decide the timing because I didn't want the tender parts to disintegrate. Sadly, when I produced the dish, dripping with butter, as an *entrée*, we could have been chewing on bits of old rope. Only the very tips were edible. We knew that asparagus should really be eaten within an hour or two of picking and this experience proved it.

After making some joint policy decisions about exactly where the loo, bidet, hand-basin and bath should go in the bathroom, I left Jack to cut pipes and solder things up all afternoon. We wanted hot water from the *chauffe-eau* to come out of taps in the kitchen and a washbasin in our bedroom before the circuit was plumbed into the bathroom equipment. This meant that Jack had to put in the feeder pipes in the bathroom and then blank them off. For once he didn't need my help to hold things or provide moral support. I painted the geranium container, drew a map to show Chantal and Georges how to find us, and then — with a clear conscience — read a book in the sun. It was bliss. *St Paradis sans bricolage* — for me, anyway.

## Chapter Fifteen – May 1998

$O$n the morning I was opening the shutters in our bedroom when I glanced to the left to the field beyond the Lebruns' house. It was a long way, but I was sure I could see a Limousin bull accompanied by his wives and a set of baby calves. I desperately hoped it was the old Bull by the Back Door. Since the beginning of 1996 we had looked in every field around St Paradis, trying to find him and he just hadn't been visible. We hoped he hadn't been sold for cat-meat.

When we were shutting the windows prior to going to collect the stainless steel flue, Jack found a little lizard which had climbed into the spare bedroom by mistake. It had been sunning itself on the windowsill and when we approached had run in panic into the room instead of down the wall. It scuttled under a crack between the skirting board and the floorboards and we couldn't find it. We didn't want it to die of starvation because the wall under the windowsill was covered in gloss paint which would be too slippery for it to climb up and find its way home. So we left the window propped open with a gangplank of wood leading up from the floor to the windowsill, to give it an escape route. As we looked at our humane handiwork we knew any Frenchman would think we were out of our minds!

When we arrived at the depot we found that the nice man's suppliers had not delivered the right bits and pieces for the chimney. We hung around while he tried to rectify the problem. He sent his assistant to another branch but when she returned some time later, things still weren't right. So he telephoned a rival company in a nearby town and arranged for us to pick up the final missing part there, exchanging it for one which had been sent by mistake. We couldn't find the shop. When we got there it was closing time and the proprietor was standing on the threshold bearing the replacement in his hand. We effected a hand-over reminiscent of an Olympic 4x400m relay team.

Before supper we walked down to the bull's field and discovered to our disappointment that it wasn't the battle-scarred veteran on the cover of "A Bull by the Back Door" but the young one

*I day-dreamed about the poor mule: we had a big field, a barn and donkey-sized stables...*

198

mentioned at the very end of the book. He was, however, by definition, one of "our" bulls, so I was pleased to see him. I took some photographs but the subject and his harem were at a distance. I tried to get him to come across and talk to me over the fragile makeshift fence by calling the Lincolnshire cow-call of "Cup! Cup!". He didn't come any closer but just glared, surrounded by his family in a defensive position. Jack was scared.

"I really don't think it's a good idea," he said, edging away. "Especially when you're wearing a bright red cardigan! He doesn't know he's famous and that you think he's a bosom pal."

Reluctantly I agreed. I wasn't frightened but the bull could have made matchsticks out of the thin wood and binder twine barrier if he had chosen to have a go at me. It didn't even have the deterrent value of an electric fence.

After supper Jack tried our e-mail. We had been afraid that we had been sending messages into thin air, but we had received some replies so we knew we were now in communication with the world. It was rather an awesome thought in such an ancient and incongruous setting. We could exchange pleasantries with Outer Mongolia but we didn't have piped hot water...

The next morning we went to the city to replenish our stocks of DIY materials and food. We were having problems with the fridge. Jack had over-ridden the thermostat so that it would work in the cold but we had forgotten to reset it for summer temperatures. Far from suffering from food poisoning because nothing was cold enough, our provisions were now coming out frozen solid and then suffering when they reached room temperature. A cucumber which had frozen and then thawed out was just liquid goo inside a green skin, the mushrooms went like golf-balls and then rotted, and the same fate had befallen various other vegetables — including brittle lettuce leaves which broke off with a crack. The eggs had fractured shells and solid insides. We were furious with ourselves. Jack readjusted the setting on the thermostat, but it was too late to save quite a lot of fresh produce.

Chantal rang to say that their car had been stolen from their garage and that they thought it was unlikely they would be able to visit us unless the police found it. The sickening thing was that the insurance company wouldn't pay because the vehicle had been parked with the keys in the ignition. The thief must have done some research beforehand. Their house was almost hidden from the rural road. From the back, you couldn't tell what sort of building it was. Chantal had been on the terrace with the children when the theft happened a few metres away. We were so sorry for them. Few of us can afford to go out and buy a replacement car straight out of the blue. It began to look as if no one was going to visit us and we waited for our Deux-Sèvres friends to ring with a disaster story, too. Fortunately, they didn't.

We got busy installing a washbasin which Roger and Eileen had given us. They had taken it out of the master bedroom in their house in York before installing an en suite bathroom. We wanted it in our St Paradis bedroom so that if we had guests we could be independent of the bathroom. We also wanted it to use now, as the bathroom was nowhere near finished. Like most jobs, fixing the washbasin was more complicated than it appeared. The two places (the *only* two places) where it needed to be screwed on to the wall turned out not to be granite but soft mortar and the screws wouldn't hold until Jack had done time-consuming things to them with Polyfilla. Then he hung a Patricia Kelsall picture of the house above the china cabinet on the landing and tidied up the hole with the remaining filler. The plaster in the house is very soft and all the previous occupants used to hang things from nails stuck into the ceiling beams and the wooden battens in the lath and plaster internal walls. Everywhere positively bristled with rusty nails when we moved in — in fact, it was hard to think what they could all have been used for!

We could smell soot in the *cantou* chimney and knew that this was supposed to mean an imminent storm. It thundered a bit at 7pm and we hoped that we wouldn't get torrential rain because of the hole in the barn roof.

Buying bread at Stoc in the morning before our friends arrived for the day, I made an embarrassing mistake in pronunciation. I asked the girl behind the counter if she had *de pain de campagne* (meaning "any/some wholemeal bread") and she thought I wanted *deux pains de campagne* ("two wholemeal loaves"). She gave me two, as big as cart-wheels and just as solid, and I was too shy to say that wasn't what I wanted. I knew it would take a week to eat them!

We had a very enjoyable day with our friends. At one point I did my party-piece of tipping my picnic chair into a hole and being left hanging on to Jack's arm at a precarious and unseemly angle. They brought us some *Pineau des Charentes* and a *tourteau fromager*, a local delicacy of a sort of lemony Madeira-type cake in a tortoise-shape, made from goats' cheese, with a skilfully burned black top. It was delicious.

After they'd gone, in the early evening, Jack got on with plumbing in the washbasin and I read a book in the study. All of a sudden there was a terrific wind and it began to rain. We brought in the parasol and table from outside and went back upstairs. Then the most tremendous electrical thunderstorm started which tripped out the electricity in the house. Enthralled, we stood in the pitch black by the windows and watched forked lightning, sheet lightning and general flashes across the sky. Each flash was almost immediately followed by a deafening clap of thunder. We were right in the middle of the storm and it was most impressive. We decided it must be one of those storms which was contained between the power lines. At the height of the rain it was whipping in vertical sheets across the garden and fields, and the little trees right near the back of the house were nearly lashed off their roots. Jack groped his way downstairs to put on the electricity and fetch the video camera. He video-ed the most spectacular lightning for about a quarter of an hour, with each flash more vivid than the last. One lit up the entire landscape in an eerie blue glow. For a fraction of a second it was as clear as daylight.

Jack had an early "go" at spraying the garden with weedkiller before tackling the plumbing next morning. Paul saw what he was doing and gave him some copper sulphate to put on the vine which grows across the front of the house. Then Hugo came over and offered us some stone from his new house. He had demolished a broken bread oven and was using some of the stones to make a flowerbed for Elisabeth. We were delighted to accept the rest to make our terrace at the back. We said we'd fetch it another time — or ask someone like Martin, with a lorry, to bring it for us.

At lunchtime Jack felt ill and went to bed to lie down for an hour or two. I blamed the weedkiller and he blamed the melon we'd had for breakfast, which had been past its best.

I made a meal for myself out of the day before's left-overs then part-tiled the wall behind the bedroom washbasin. I was going to leave a gap for a mirror which we had downstairs but decided it wouldn't be big enough. We would have to buy another. The tiling was not a pleasure because the old wall was so uneven that it was impossible to get all the tiles on the same plane. I expect Jack could have done it, but I am not blessed with his dogged patience.

Then I indulged myself with some more reading. We had some bookshelves in the loo which I stocked from charity shops in Northwich, rarely paying more than £1 for a book and more usually about 45p. I didn't like to leave expensive new books in the house when it was unoccupied because the pages went wavy.

I finished a crime novel and then turned to a recent purchase: a fascinating account of what women in the *département* had done for the Resistance*. It made sobering reading. One or two were glamorous and brave secret-agent types, others were Communists who risked their lives for their politics (a large part of the Resistance, which was split into three factions, was Communist), several had husbands who were prisoners of war and wanted to strike back at the Germans, but mostly they were very ordinary, very courageous women of all ages — from teenagers to grandmothers — who like my Aunt Helen had got roped into the war accidentally as a result of patriotism and because they wanted to help the *gars* (young lads) in the Maquis who were evading forced labour in Germany. The stories were very human. Several stuck in my mind.

Things seemed to have gone especially crazy around 7 June 1944 (the day after D-Day) when the *département*'s capital was prematurely liberated by the Resistance — and then recaptured a few days later by reinforced German troops with very nasty results. In the time of euphoria, the previously collaborating officers, NCOs and trainee soldiers from the *Ecole de la Garde* in the city went over

*Femmes de la Résistance en Creuse, by Marc Parrotin, Editions Verso, 1997 ISBN 2.903870.82.9

to the Resistance (which had previously been busy killing them). On June 9 one poor farmer's wife discovered about 80 of them on her doorstep, plus 30 German prisoners they had taken. She was expected to provide food for them all. They killed four sheep the first day, a calf the next and something I couldn't translate (probably a gelding) on the third. The officers organised a feast to celebrate their victory and foolishly — but perhaps understandably — invited their counterparts in the nearby Resistance groups to attend. They had just finished the meal when they were all encircled by German troops and captured: with dire consequences for most. The farmer and his wife were spared because the German prisoners said they had been treated well by them, but their farmhouse and farm buildings were destroyed as a reprisal. It was not until August 25 that the capital was permanently liberated.

Another woman was the middle-aged widowed chatelaine of a 12th century hilltop castle from where she ran a big farm. Her late husband had been a senator for the *département* between 1907-24 and mayor of a local town. She supported the Maquis, took risks and participated actively in the Resistance movement. On July 17 the Maquis in her area captured a high-ranking German officer and his driver and shut them up in the tower of her castle. Then they went away and left her alone to guard the prisoners! The Germans found out where they were and came to get them, accusing the poor woman of having captured them herself. She was being taken away to the prison where captives were being sorted out into those who were to be executed and those destined for concentration camps, when some French fighters from the Garde Mobile popped up and shot the officer next to her dead — then disappeared. Once again, she was accused, this time of killing an officer! She was in a fragile state of health but the soldiers manhandled her roughly, although she pleaded that she wasn't armed and couldn't possibly have killed anyone. Then she was beaten up and taken to the prison by lorry, the body of the dead officer at her feet. She was kept in prison for three days and subjected to numerous interrogations. Eventually she so impressed her inquisitors that they let her go free for lack of evidence. She arrived home exhausted, having walked the 12 kilometres back to her castle through a deserted landscape, with no one to help her. Her captors had taunted her: "Go back to your *château*, Madame, and we will come tomorrow to burn it down and you with it." But they didn't carry out the threat.

Later she and her family erected a granite memorial, honouring three soldiers from the Garde who had died in a separate incident nearby on July 17 and commemorating the other tragic events of that day. She was marked for life emotionally by what had happened and in her last years made a daily pilgrimage to the stone monument.

Some women escaped discovery. A night-duty telephonist earned the Croix de Guerre for intercepting enemy phone calls from 1943 onwards and passing on valuable information to the Resistance. She was said to have saved numerous lives.

Others were not so lucky. A miller and his wife provided flour and a refuge for young men in the nearby Maquis group who were hiding in the countryside. They were denounced. The miller was arrested by the Gestapo, tortured, imprisoned for a short time at Limoges (from where he wrote his wife a last letter) and deported to a camp in Germany. His wife, who was left destitute with six children, sent two parcels to the prison at Limoges but never heard from him again. He died a year later, about five weeks before the end of the war.

I spent hours reading the book with the aid of a dictionary for the unfamiliar words. I felt it would be disrespectful to miss out any of the 128 women who were featured.

By midnight Jack had done all the hot and cold pipework and we tried out the cold water in the back kitchen and bedroom washbasin. Unfortunately there were leaks in the most unexpected places: the pressure gauge downstairs and one of the compression joints under the *chauffe-eau* in the bathroom. Jack fixed them and we went to bed at 1am with a certain sense of achievement.

The following day we went shopping again, did some more plumbing and then went over to Paul's for a drink. Elisabeth had been called out to accompany her daughter on a car trip so Paul was on his own in the garden doing the Tiercé. We sat down on the terrace with him in the sunshine and chatted for an hour and a half, demolishing a nice bottle of *rouge* in the process. Paul explained that his doctor said a drop of *un bon Bordeaux* would be good for his health. This was a lucky coincidence since Paul had always thought that a very large drop did him no end of good. How nice to have a doctor who agreed!

Jack showed him my Internet website on the laptop computer and he was suitably and politely impressed, though I am not sure that our French was up to explaining exactly what we were demonstrating.

Back home, plumbing dominated our thoughts and activities until bedtime. We now had the *chauffe-eau* connected electrically and it was busy heating 150 litres of water. Unfortunately it took too long to warm up such a large volume for us to have any hot water to wash in before we went to bed.

We got up early because we couldn't contain our curiosity about the water. We turned on the tap over the sink in the back kitchen and water gushed out — piping hot. Too hot, in fact, although it was exactly 60°C as recommended. We had to adjust the mixer tap to get it to a comfortable temperature without rubber gloves. We took photos and video-ed each other turning on the tap and watching the water running down the plug-hole. Anyone would have thought we were mad — but we knew Marguerite would have understood. To be released from the drudgery of having to heat water in the kettle and a large saucepan on the gas stove, and risk a severe scalding by carrying it to wherever it was needed for each little task, was absolutely wonderful. We could hardly believe it after four years at St Paradis.

After breakfast I celebrated by washing my hair in the luxury of the back kitchen. It was so easy! Normally it was a convoluted and long-winded nuisance which tended to be put off until I looked as though I was cultivating rats' tails on my head.

I put insulating foam around the pipes under the working surface in the kitchen so that we didn't have to run off much water before it became hot. Jack did the same on the pipes in the bathroom. We watched the electricity meter whizzing round like nobody's business, but we just didn't care.

Michel had said that the village workman strimmed the verges in St Paradis on the 18th of the month and he was right. Next day the chap was at it bright and early. The weather was hot again, though a cool breeze stopped it being quite as stifling as before, and we felt sorry for the poor man working in ear defenders, mask, apron, wellingtons and gloves, with the motor for the strimmer strapped on his back. Jack gets "vibration white finger" after a fairly short time with our strimmer and he wondered if the professional also suffered from it. The workman was conscientious. He started while we were having our breakfast, stopped for a short time at noon when Paul and Michel invited him in for a drink and then carried on again until it was all done in mid-afternoon. He had a special device which blew the cut grass off the road and back on to the verges to stop it being a traffic hazard.

We were saved a morning trip to the town to buy some bread when the mobile bread shop appeared outside. I went out for our usual ordinary *pain* (I think we had reluctantly thrown away the extra *pain de campagne* which had soon acquired the consistency of cast-iron). Michel and Charles were there too and I apologised for my more than usually awful working gear. We had seriously dirty work to do.

We had meant to bring the pressure washer from England so that we could fix on the sand-blasting attachment and have a go at the *cantou*. We cursed ourselves for forgetting it. We wanted to get the fireplace as clean as possible before we installed the beautiful big Godin. At the very beginning, Marguerite had told me firmly that she didn't want the fireplace cleaned so thoroughly that it lost its character. It's smoky deposits represented 200 years of family history. We had promised to respect this wish. But she raised no objections to it being cleaned superficially. I scrubbed the soot-blackened stones with a wire brush and was pleased that it made an appreciable difference. Instead of being shiny black with carbon deposits and distinctly unappealing, the granite was now matt dark brown and much more attractive. I tried scrubbing one stone with a brush and diluted Flash but what I gained in washing off the soot I lost in scrubbing the soot solution into the stone itself. The water was filthy. Jack scraped the chimney with a spade and got down quite a lot of carbon, but nothing like the amount we produced when we did it a few years before. By everyday standards we hadn't used the fireplace much and hadn't created much of a deposit up there.

Jack measured exactly where the stove would go and then cemented into place two stones he had cut to size in England to take the Godin's front feet. They were too wide for the existing hearthstone, which projected out into the room. The stones had been taken from the remains of the burnt house but they were clean instead of sooty and looked rather obvious. We would have to wait for them to get dirty and blend in.

We continued to work on various house projects during the day and in the early evening walked over to the wood to look for dead trees which we could mark out for cutting down in the New Year. We went via the newest little oak tree at the bottom of the field which we watered with a bucket of water from the nearby duck pond. Sadly, without The Duck with the Dirty Laugh and his friends, the pond was covered with duckweed, looked stagnant and smelled revolting. There were no visible frogs either. We knew they were still there somewhere because we could hear them croaking in chorus at night.

When we reached the wood we found it was a monument to fecundity and lack of human intervention. Even the apparently barren trees, which in January we had ear-marked for chopping down had some branches bearing leaves. In half an acre, we could only find one paltry tree which wasn't hale and hearty, so it looked as if Jack's lumberjack ambitions might have to go on hold for another year.

While we were there I continued my verbal campaign to construct a gas barbecue which we had bought with credit card points the previous summer (it was the only thing in the catalogue that we fancied) and which was still in its box in the salon. Its list price was £90 but we must have spent thousands earning the points to get it! My main argument was that the only food we had left in the fridge was designed to be barbecued, had been bought with it in mind and wouldn't be half as nice done with a griddle on the gas stove. Jack had been resisting the wifely campaign for a week on the grounds that he was far too busy doing important things to bother with such trivialities as assembling a barbecue.

Eventually he buckled under the strain and agreed to put it

together. I argued that for a man of his ability it would be a task of a few minutes.

When we opened the box at 8.20pm he discovered it was much more complicated to assemble than we had thought. This was a pain in one respect but good in that it presented him with a practical challenge which he couldn't refuse. It was daylight and he was in shirt-sleeves when he started; it was pitch black and he was in a thick sweater by the time he finished at 10pm. By the light of the halogen lamp which illuminates the back garden we ate our barbecued kebabs and sausages at 10.20pm surrounded by inky darkness, to the amusement of the neighbours, no doubt. It worried me that less knowledgeable *bricoleurs*, without years of experience as physical chemists building complicated experimental rigs, might have bodged together a very dangerous piece of equipment instead of an innocent gas barbecue.

Afterwards we connected to the Internet for our nightly trawl for messages. It was very reassuring to be in touch with our neighbours, who were dealing with the book orders for me (and could pass on news about Mother and Auntie), and with Chris and Linda. The computer crashed when we were trying to retrieve our mail. Jack spent ages getting it going again. Although we were very tired, we thought there might be something important in the e-mail.

We finally got the message: "Introducing the Fastest, Easiest, and Safest Way For YOU to Make Thousands of Dollars in Record Breaking Time with no personal selling! I started making money my first week and so can YOU!"

It was junk mail. What's called "Spam" on the Internet and is as welcome as all the advertising bumf that comes through the letterbox these days. It's usually full of spelling mistakes and works on the assumption that the recipients are incredibly stupid and incredibly greedy. What a waste of effort! We went to bed.

The next day passed happily. Jack bought himself an electric tile cutter with a diamond tipped cutting disk, Jan and Beatrice came for a convivial supper (sadly, without the dogs, as the young one was on heat), the bathroom came on slowly and steadily — and I impaled my ankle on a short (but sharp!) stake which we had used to mark out where the terrace would go one day. It made a nasty mess and I didn't have a plaster big enough to cover the deep graze and puncture hole. As I lay awake that night with a throbbing ankle, I was furious with myself for forgetting the stake was there.

The following day, May 20th, was market day and we decided to go into the nearest town for our shopping. We had been reminded about it when Michel came round to Paul's in his best clothes, saying he was off to the *foire*. We immediately jumped to the conclusion that he meant "funfair" until we realised that the word also referred to the more traditional "fair", as in "market", and it was, of course, the 20th. We wished they had a more memorable system, such as holding the market on the first and third Tuesday of the month...

First we went to the post office to send a letter to Mother about what we had been doing. I also wanted to buy a book of self-adhesive stamps for other letters. I couldn't remember the word for "book of stamps", which I knew didn't translate literally, so I took an empty one with me so that I could point to it and say: "I want one of these, please".

I can't remember ever having a quick transaction in this post office, charming though the personnel are. It's a stylish building with lots of glass and some modern art which I'm certain the PO would never have shelled out for in England. That's the difference between French public buildings and ours. They believe that aesthetics are important, even in the most mundane surroundings, and we don't.

There was a long queue for the two serving windows when we arrived and a woman standing at the right-hand position was getting the clerk to telephone someone on her behalf. I couldn't think why she hadn't called whoever it was on her own phone from home. The counter clerk's abortive attempts went on for ages, much to the tut-tutting of the rest of the French people in the queue, until he said rather tartly that the number she had given him was a fax number and he couldn't help her any further. The next person in the queue actually wanted to send a fax — a service advertised on a poster by the door — and was horrified when she discovered that it would cost her over 40FF. The clerk disappeared for some time and sent the message.

When it was my turn I waved my book of stamps around and asked for a similar one. I would have been quite happy with ten basic stamps instead but I couldn't remember offhand how much they cost. The woman who was serving me said something that I didn't catch and also disappeared into the nether regions where there appeared to be a sorting office. She left the door ajar and I could see her searching through drawers and cupboards. She must have been gone five minutes and I began to feel exasperated: all I wanted was some stamps and the whole thing was getting out of hand. The queue behind me was not happy. She eventually came back with a big brand-new book containing probably a hundred sheets of the latest batch of colourful commemorative stamps, and asked if I would like to have some of these instead. They were newly issued that day, she was very proud of them, and she thought I might like to send them to England as a special treat. I forgot my earlier impatience and thanked her profusely for going to such much trouble for a foreigner.

Our little transaction over we walked down to the market in search of vegetables and cheese. By accident we had discovered some heavenly, salty "St Chabrais" cheese on our Stoc delicatessen counter, but we had never been able to find it anywhere else. We knew it came from a local farm and hoped the proprietors might deal with one of the *fromagers* on the market. I read the name tags on each cheese on every stall but couldn't track it down. By this time I was determined not to go home empty-handed, so I bought something that looked white and interesting on a little stall run by a farmer's wife. She put it in a plastic bag for me and warned me not to let it get upside down because all the whey would spill out. I should have been warned. I like my cheese mature rather than embryonic! We had it for lunch and it really didn't taste of anything.

That afternoon I did the washing in our 1950s washing machine and 1960s spin drier, *using hot water from the tap* to fill the washer. I was prepared for the whole thing to be doddle for a change and was probably too complacent. I was in heaven until (i) I discovered that the paddle had jammed (ii) the spin drier leapt away from me in an unbalanced frenzy and spewed soapy water all over the back kitchen (iii) a paper hankie in a sweatshirt pocket disintegrated and contaminated the last load of washing and (iv) the soggy shreds of paper floating in the dirty water jammed the filter constantly as I was emptying the machine so it took four times longer than usual. The experience wasn't as much fun as I had expected.

Ascension Day, May 21: I looked out of the study window before breakfast and spotted a new resident in the field beyond ours. For days there had been six pregnant cows in there. Now there were five pregnant cows, a proud mum and a newborn calf, tottering round on unsteady long legs and keeping close to the milk bar. He was gorgeous.

Chantal rang to say they had bought another car and would be along to see us as planned, bringing another of our friends from Mornant who would be very interested to see the house. I grouted the tiles above the washbasin in our bedroom, where we had now fixed a new big mirror. And we had a welcome visitor — Monique, the daughter of our late neighbour who had been Marguerite's friend and who had owned Betty the dog. She and her family came to St Paradis every weekend to stay in her mother's old house. They had adopted Betty and she had always come too — until we spotted during a previous holiday that she was no longer around. Monique told us sadly that Betty had died of an infection, aged only nine, and that the whole family missed her terribly. I promised to give them a copy of one of Patricia Kelsall's drawings from "A Bull by the Back Door" which showed Betty in her favourite place — lying in the middle of the road waiting for something exciting to happen.

In her turn, Monique had brought us a present. It was a colour photograph of Marguerite, aged about 80, in widow's weeds, walking up from our house to pay a social call on Monique's mother. We were fascinated to see that the burned house was still intact. From the parts of the shell which remained when we bought it, we had never been able to visualise how it had once looked. Now we knew. Monique said her grandmother had lived there. We realised that, when she married, Monique's mother had moved all of 50 feet down the road from where she was born — and she had lived in that spot more or less until she died.

We showed Monique around the house, which she had not explored since Marguerite's death. She said that when she was young she often came to have coffee with Marguerite, and agreed with the Martins that the kitchen had been very dark. Our would-be bathroom had been a bedroom and (as we thought) the marks on the wall had been caused by a bedstead. In Marguerite's later years, when she spent the summers at St Paradis, Monique's mother had slept in a bed near her at night in case she needed anything.

Marguerite had obviously dearly loved the house where she had been so happy as a girl. She had brought young people back into it — we remembered Georges also saying that he had been a frequent visitor as a little boy. We felt happy, and humble, to have been able to revitalise it for her. We still believed very strongly that she had somehow chosen us to do this. Perhaps she had sensed that our sons would help us to make it a happy family home again.

In the beginning it had felt as if she was lending the house to us but as time wore on it had become more and more our own, as we spruced up, decorated and furnished all the different parts. I now no longer had a subconscious desire to place my hand in hers and ask her to show me round and reveal its secrets. When I looked at photographs of what we had tackled when we bought the property I could hardly believe that we had been so brave. At the time, it had seemed the most natural thing in the world.

That evening we poured self-levelling compound, *enduit de sol autoglissant*, over the bathroom floor as a foundation for the ceramic floor tiles we had bought two years before in a mad rush of optimism. It was supposed to be one of the defining DIY moments in the history of the house renovation and Jack had been looking forward to it for weeks. The instructions, which we followed minutely, said that the stuff should end up flat. We had expected it to have the consistency of water, but it was more like sludge. It sat like a lump of grey blancmange in the middle of the bathroom floor and didn't do anything. Jack was not prepared for this. We had not constructed any shuttering on the floor which could be used to level it. We had just made frames for the bath, *chauffe-eau* cupboard and other equipment and had expected the *enduit de sol* to flow neatly up to the bases. He frantically tried to level it with a trowel before it dried. In the morning it resembled the South Downs and Jack was inconsolable. Self-levelling it was not.

We decided to go to the *départemental* capital to buy some more, to pour a thin skim over the top. We had bought the original sack of levelling compound in the city but when we went to the same DIY franchise in the capital, they didn't have any. Jack was determined that master craftsman Georges should not see such a bodged job, so we searched the area frantically for a builder's merchant who might stock the stuff. One, which advertised in the Yellow Pages, was on the suburban outskirts where a tiny circus was camped out in the most surrealistic fashion. A spotted Appaloosa pony was tethered beside a bus stop and there was a llama on the opposite side of the road eating someone's hedge. The builder's merchant didn't have any *enduit de sol* — though I have a horrible suspicion that my pronunciation had wandered off and I actually asked for *endroit de sol*, which is pretty meaningless but could perhaps be translated as "floor the right way up". They didn't have any of that, either!

We were desperate by lunchtime — Jack had a reputation to protect, after all — so we decided to drive to another town, south of where we lived, to see if the DIY store there had any *enduit de sol*. The route from the capital took us past where the poor woman had catered for 80 *gardes* and had her farm destroyed for her pains. The shop not only had a profusion of *enduit de sol*, it had a special offer on it and we paid 59FF for 25 kilos instead of 143FF.

Back home we carried on trying to make the place look civilised for the visit of the Mornantais. We struggled to lift the big Godin off its wheeled trolley and on to the hearthstones which Jack had widened to take its feet. The stove fitted perfectly and, with the first metre of its stainless steel flue popped temporarily in place, looked wonderfully in keeping with the ancient fireplace (see drawing on page 154). We were sure that Marguerite would be pleased. We kept the little Godin beside it as our main source of heat until the new *poêle* could be installed properly.

Paul and Elisabeth came round for supper that night. We had a lovely evening together and were just sipping post-dinner coffee when there was a knock at the door. It was Mme Echelle, plus our old friend Gitane and the very timid Soupette. We invited Madame in to join us for coffee and the dogs came too. It was the first time Soupette had dared to come into the kitchen — she usually backed away from us, whining, with her tail between her legs. That response always upset Jack in particular, because he hated animals to be afraid of him. She obviously felt secure because her mistress had endorsed our house and from that moment onwards she visited several times a day, growing in confidence over the coming months until she thought nothing of jumping on to our knees when we sat on the sofa during the evening and falling asleep across our laps. From being the most frightened dog in St Paradis, when faced by *les anglais*, she became the most at ease.

We all chatted and swapped news. Then Paul and Elisabeth saw a car stopping near their house. Paul went out to see who it was and found it was his youngest daughter and her husband, whom we like very much. We invited them in, too, and they joined in the conversation round the big kitchen table, accepting a cup of coffee and a *peu de rouge* respectively. Everyone settled down and made themselves at home. We were delighted that we had enough wine, coffee, nibbles, glassware, crockery and chairs to entertain friends who arrived at random in the real French way. We couldn't put our fingers on why it wasn't an "English" gathering. Perhaps because we all sat round the table, close to one another, rather than being spread out around a sitting room as our guests would have been at home in Hartford. Indeed, we would have been hard-pressed to have seated more than five comfortably at any given time in Cheshire. At St Paradis there was still an empty chair at the 8ft-long kitchen table and we could have squeezed in a few more if necessary. It felt good.

Later, when everyone had gone, I tackled a mountain of washing up and Jack mixed the new batch of *enduit de sol*. It was much thinner than the other compound, although he made it up to the same specifications. It flowed in like water and we had an instant flat floor in the bathroom. Honour was appeased and Jack went to bed a happy man.

As our last full day at St Paradis began, we noted that the weather was changing. There was a cold wind from the north which made the hot balmy days of the previous fortnight just a pleasant memory.

Chantal, Georges and our friend Claude arrived at 10.15am after a drive from Mornant which usually took us three hours. Chantal, bless her, had been up at 6am to make us a *clafoutis* (fresh cherries cooked in batter) for pudding. They also brought some pretty handmade boiled sweets and some mouth-watering chocolate from the *chocolatier* in Mornant. I had just put a leg of lamb in the oven to roast, shamelessly adapting Eileen's favourite recipe which uses garlic, rosemary and lots of melted redcurrant jelly. I was not, however, going to own up to the jelly, since the French think it is a very odd English aberration to eat "jam" with meat.

We showed them round. Claude particularly wanted to look at our unspoilt traditional farmhouse. She was delighted with the contraption under the kitchen window and said it was very rare. Her grandmother had had one and Claude confirmed what others had said, that it was designed to keep food warm. You put hot embers in trays on the brick shelf under the tiled top with its two metal grilles, placed your saucepans or stewpots on top of the grilles, and left them to heat gently until it was mealtime.

I was banking on buying some fresh bread for lunch from the mobile *boulangerie*. We were in the attic showing our friends the "museum-pieces" up there when I heard the familiar hoot from the van. I raced down the various flights of stairs and rushed out, panting, to the stopping place. It was the butcher in a new white van. I felt a fool and went back up into the attic. A few minutes later there was another hoot. I repeated the procedure. This time it was the cheese merchant, in a new white van. Embarrassed (I was after all supposed to be a knowledgeable resident of St Paradis who knew all about the timetable of the travelling shops) I climbed back up to the attic empty-handed. Then there was another hoot. I tried again. It was the baker, in a new white van. I bought my bread.

We had never had three mobile shops calling on a Saturday morning in such quick succession. The traders usually had a white van, a grey one and a red one. Now they appeared to have indistinguishable new white ones. Had there been a special offer at the white van shop? Had the shopkeepers increased the number of their visits in order to pay for the vehicles? It was very confusing. Months later I still go out, six francs in hand, to buy my *pain* from the wrong *camionnette*.

We walked round part of the village and Mme Echelle's son gave us the keys to the church. I was suddenly moved to take a whole film of photographs of it for posterity and went back home to fetch my camera while the others inspected the stencilling and the paintings. Michel was on his vegetable garden and I stopped to explain what I was doing. He said, as he had done almost exactly two years before when we had first discovered the beauty of the church, that it was the feast of the little bishop the following day. I hoped the saint was pleased that Michel remembered him so faithfully year in, year out. His "day" had once been the highlight of the village's social and religious life. Did the church have some sort of spiritual or emotional pull which attracted us to it at this time of the year? We passed it every day that we were at St Paradis, after all, but rarely actually went in. It seemed somehow fitting that I should take the photographs now. I was delighted with them when they were developed and printed, for the flash had revealed details which were impossible to see in the gloomy light inside the building.

Lunch lasted a long time, in the best French fashion. The lamb, with its secret ingredient, was a hit. Then we went for a walk the other way round the village and stopped to talk to the agricultural contractor's uncle who lived next door to Guy and Virginie (they were in Lyon at the time). He said our field would soon be ready to cut for hay; afterwards they would put cattle in it and later horses, to eat what the cattle didn't like so that nothing was wasted. That explained the horse droppings we found every year!

We wandered on, skirting a pond where none of the placid ducks had a dirty laugh, and passing the back of the former priest's house where we discovered a field full of nanny goats and kids, watched over by a big billygoat with an enormous beard. We hadn't seen them there before. Goats were rare in St Paradis.

Gitane, Soupette, Max and Milord tumbled out of the old *auberge* in a vociferous welcome, following us up the road in the hope of some left-over scraps from lunch. We shoo-ed them away. Canine friends came after human friends in the pecking order. They could have their little feast later.

Back home, we sat out in the back garden while Jack did the washing up. Chantal joked that it would never occur to a French husband to do such a chore. It was sunny but the north wind was still pretty fresh. Our friends were sensibly wearing jackets but I was just in a sweater and felt the chill. At about 6pm they started to indicate that they should leave, and they actually went at 6.45pm. We couldn't persuade them to stay for supper: they said that if they were hungry they'd make a quick stop on the return journey.

Their new car was three years old and had the same mileage on the clock as the stolen one. It was an attractive dark metallic green which changed colour according to the light but it had been a very unwelcome expense.

As we waved them off, we thought what fun it had been to entertain our special friends in our very own French house. It was good to have a legitimate stake in their homeland and to feel that it was ours, too. They rarely came to England because the trip was so difficult, but St Paradis was only three hours away from Mornant — probably less when Georges was behind the wheel! Situated as we were, in the very centre of our adopted country, we felt that our Mornant friends and our scattered French "family" were all within easy reach.

Wanting to leave the land neat before we set off for Cheshire the following day, Jack mowed the grass out at the back. I went up to the study and composed my diary on the computer, fortified by a glass or two of Jameson's duty-free whiskey.

At the end of the day's entry I wrote: "What a wonderful holiday! The house really feels ours now: Marguerite has definitely handed it over to us with her blessing. We are surrounded by friends and we feel perfectly at home. What more could you ask for? I wouldn't be a tourist for all the tea in China."

# Some of the French-based books
# published by the Léonie Press:

A BULL BY THE BACK
DOOR
by ANNE LOADER

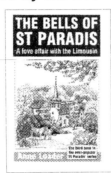

THE BELLS OF ST PARADIS
by ANNE LOADER
ISBN 1 901253 26 0   £9.99

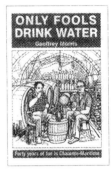

ONLY FOOLS DRINK WATER
by GEOFFREY MORRIS
ISBN 1 901253 10 4   £8.99

BON COURAGE, MES AMIS!
by SHEILA WRIGHT
ISBN 1 901253  30 9  £8.99

OU EST LE 'PING'?
by GRACE McKEE
ISBN 1 901253 11 2   £7.99

BUTTERFLIES ON MIMOSA
by ELEANOR FRANCIS
ISBN 1 901253 23 6  £8.99

BANANAS IN BORDEAUX
LOUISE FRANKLIN CASTANET
ISBN 1 901253 29 5  £10.99

POLLY TAKES THE SCENIC
ROUTE by GAY PYPER
ISBN 1 901253 33 3  £8.99

THE HIDDEN TRIANGLE
A French Odyssey
by VALERIE THOMPSON